PUSHKIN PRESS CLASSICS

CONVERSATIONS WITH RILKE

'A creative spirit and a friend to all creative spirits… an ornament to literary France… an artist with words, lovable and worthy of love'
THOMAS MANN

'The Betz translation of The Notebooks of Malte Laurids Brigge constituted a conversation, even a confidence… a translation from heart to heart'
JEAN CASSOU

MAURICE BETZ (1898–1946), as well as writing poetry and novels, was a prolific translator of Friedrich Nietzsche, Stefan Zweig and Thomas Mann. He worked closely with Rilke on the French translations of his works while Rilke was alive, and continued translating the poet into French in the decades following his death. He fought in both World Wars and was made a prisoner in the Second. Shortly after the war, he was found dead in a hotel room in Tours, having asked for an early wake-up call.

WILL STONE is a poet, essayist and literary translator of French, Franco-Belgian and German literature. His previous translations include *Rilke in Paris*, also by Maurice Betz, several works by Stefan Zweig, and poems by Georg Trakl and Rainer Maria Rilke, all available from Pushkin Press.

CONVERSATIONS WITH RILKE

MAURICE BETZ

TRANSLATED FROM THE FRENCH
BY WILL STONE

PUSHKIN PRESS CLASSICS

Pushkin Press
Somerset House, Strand
London WC2R 1LA

English translation © Will Stone 2025

Conversations with Rilke was first published as
Rilke vivant by Émile-Paul in Paris, 1937

First published by Pushkin Press in 2025

1 3 5 7 9 8 6 4 2

ISBN 13: 978-1-80533-028-8

All rights reserved. No part of this publication may be reproduced,
stored in a retrieval system or transmitted in any form or by any
means, electronic, mechanical, photocopying, recording or otherwise,
without prior permission in writing from Pushkin Press

Cover: *The Boulevard Viewed from Above*, 1880, by Gustave Caillebotte

Designed and typeset by Tetragon, London

Printed and bound in the United Kingdom by Clays Ltd, Elcograf S.p.A.

www.pushkinpress.com

CONVERSATIONS
WITH RILKE

Maurice Betz on the fifth-floor balcony at 1, rue de Médicis, Paris

Contents

Introduction		*ix*
Translator's Note		*xxiii*
	On the Discovery of Rilke	1
I	*The Book of Images*, Civilization, 500,000 Shells	7
II	Dada, Malraux, Cocteau, Harden	14
III	First Letters from Muzot	22
IV	Paris, the French Language, Berg am Irchel	30
V	Émile-Paul, Jaloux, Benveniste	41
VI	*Les Cahiers du mois*, Sternheim, Valéry	55
VII	The Luxembourg, the Hôtel Biron, Muzot	63
VIII	Mornings Working on *The Notebooks of Malte*	71
IX	The Lost Pages of *The Notebooks of Malte*	81
X	In the Environs of the Princess	91
XI	Lou Andreas-Salomé, Gorki, Tolstoy	98
XII	Rodin, de Max, Isadora Duncan	106
XIII	Roses, Cats and Dogs	114
XIV	Bettina von Arnim, Lina Poletti and Eleonora Duse	120
XV	Giraudoux, Gide, Max Picard	127
XVI	Spain, Provence, Venice	135
XVII	*'Fate has these holes where we disappear'*	143
XVIII	*Malte, Vergers, Reconnaissance à Rilke*	151
XIX	The Last Summer of Rainer Maria Rilke	162
	Rilke Alive	168
Maurice Betz—A Poet and Literary Translator in Paris		175
Translator's Acknowledgements		179
Notes		181

Introduction

'Paris afforded Rilke a feeling of firmness, lending a certain clarity to his form, of which he also became aware in the presence of the work of Rodin. Ultimately, Paris and France were for him a landscape of the human…'

MAURICE BETZ

I

Though a gifted writer in his own right, Maurice Betz (1898–1946) is best known today as the most celebrated translator of Rainer Maria Rilke into French. Betz was fortunate to be alive at the same time as his author and in the same city, so was able to spend crucial hours in his company working on the manuscript that would further endorse Rilke's name in the Parisian literary world and beyond. Over long weeks in the spring of 1925, Betz received the poet almost daily at his home on rue de Médicis, romantically sited opposite the north-east corner of the Jardin du Luxembourg, to discuss the manuscript of Rilke's great prose work, informed by his former years in Paris, *The Notebooks of Malte Laurids Brigge*, first published in German in 1910. Following Rilke's death on 29 December 1926, Betz honoured the memory of his friend with many further translations of his poetry, essays, stories and letters.

In 1937, to commemorate the tenth anniversary of Rilke's death, Betz published, under the title *Rilke vivant, souvenirs, lettres, entretiens*, memories of his correspondence and regular meetings with Rilke during the spring of 1925. *Rilke vivant* was published by Émile-Paul

Frères, based at 14, rue de l'Abbaye in the sixth arrondissement of Paris, a publishing house that sadly no longer exists but will be forever linked to the name of Rilke in French translation. During the inter-war years Betz became the in-house editor and advisor to Émile-Paul for translations from the German language. By 1937 Émile-Paul had racked up an impressive list of Rilke in translation. From the landmark appearance of *Les Cahiers de Malte Laurids Brigge* in 1926, Betz supplied a raft of further translations, with almost one Rilke appearing annually until the year of his death. He also undertook the translation of the important memoirs *Souvenirs sur Rainer Maria Rilke*, by Princess Marie von Thurn und Taxis, which appeared with Émile-Paul in 1936, and supplemented *Rilke vivant* with his *Rilke à Paris*, which appeared in 1939.

But in the whole Betz corpus, *Rilke vivant* occupies a special place in that it reveals the conversations between translator and writer not just on the manuscript they were painstakingly honing that early spring of 1925, as the trees began to bud in the nearby Jardin du Luxembourg, but on the most varied and unexpected subjects, which were the fruit of their evolving camaraderie and mutual trust. These memoirs constitute a window on to Rilke's daily life strolling his *quartier*, the avenues of the Luxembourg, the warren of streets around it and down to the Seine. Despite its evident significance, *Rilke vivant* lay inexplicably dormant for a staggering eighty-five years before being sensibly republished in 2022 by the publisher Arfuyen as *Conversations avec Rilke*, the title we have retained for the English edition. The final unnumbered chapter of the *Conversations*, a sort of epilogue, retains the title 'Rilke Alive'. Arfuyen is at pains to draw attention to the fact that this was a crucial work in the canon of Rilke secondary literature, too long overlooked and providing a unique insight into Rilke's final Parisian sojourn of 1925.

INTRODUCTION

On 15th January 1925, Rilke finally returned to the city which had informed some of his greatest works in the decade or so before the First World War. He settled in at the Hôtel Foyot, itself now a legend as the hotel in which Joseph Roth camped out in the 1930s. He would later pen a mournful eulogy as he watched it being demolished from a café terrace on the other side of the rue de Tournon. The Foyot was perfect for Rilke, as it was close to his beloved Jardin du Luxembourg. It was also ideal as it happened to be a short walk from the apartment of his young translator Maurice Betz. But Betz does not lead us swiftly to this long-awaited rendezvous with Rilke in the shadow of the Luxembourg. Rather, in the early chapters he sets the scene for the oncoming fellowship in Paris, allowing the reader to become better acquainted with Maurice Betz, the youthful writer from Alsace who, like many a sensitive young man at age seventeen, is seduced by Rilke's work and faithfully carries a battered copy of *The Book of Images* (not the *Cornet* like the majority!) in his knapsack through the Battles of Aisne and the Marne. This youthful devotion bleeds into the post-1918 literary world of Paris, the shock of the devastating conflict placing urgent demands on young writers, the new more experimental writing emerging around the prolific spirit of Marcel Arland and the Stock publishing house run by Florent Fels.

In these pages we are treated to an intimate view of the long-since-vanished world of the literary cottage industry within which Betz was deeply embedded, a trusted advisor on German literature who worked his niche and was respected as a specialist. Betz makes his tentative entry as a writer with the poetry collection *Scaferlati pour troupes* (1921), and we are informed of the dizzying rise of new reviews, led by Fels's journal *Les Contemporains*, and on its heels François Berge's *Les Cahiers du mois*, all attempting to showcase and contextualize the new, more provocative French and international writing. Here are names who no longer figure, others who have endured, a few now viewed as literary cornerstones. Passing through the anecdotes and stories are the likes of the heavyweights, Malraux, Aragon, Gide, Cocteau, Giraudoux, then the up-and-coming Mac Orlan, Edmond Jaloux, Emmanuel Bove, Raymond Radiguet. Betz relishes summoning these ghosts and resurrecting their interplay, almost as if he is, even by 1937, memorializing a period whose sap is spent. The recollection of acerbic wisecracking German playwright Carl Sternheim attempting to conquer Paris with his family in tow is particularly piquant, revealing Betz as a subtle writer and perceptive observer. This blackly humorous portrait segues into the long-anticipated first meeting with Sternheim's antithesis, Rilke, in the vestibule of the Foyot.

II

This first meeting with Rilke in Paris in early 1925 is the result of a correspondence which began with Betz pluckily writing to Rilke over the winter of 1922–23 to gain permission to translate an excerpt from *The Notebooks of Malte Laurids Brigge*, for inclusion in a special issue of *Les Contemporains*. From his chosen sequestration, the remote Château de Muzot in the Valais region of Switzerland, Rilke replies positively. This is not a given, since Rilke is very particular about who translates his work and even more so into French, his most treasured language. However, he had been impressed with the poems in Betz's *Scaferlati pour troupes*, which the young translator had gamely included with his appeal. Furthermore, Betz, without his knowledge, has also been recommended to Rilke as an able translator from German by one Inga Junghanns, a singer who had not only once performed for Rilke but also had taken it upon herself to translate the *Notebooks* into her native Danish. Rilke is further persuaded when Betz's translated excerpt in *Les Contemporains* reaches his hands in July 1923 and appears to honour the original. Endorsed by his author, an exuberant Betz is keen to proceed and translate the remainder of the *Notebooks*, which hitherto had only received the attention of André Gide.

The relationship between Rilke and Gide is worthy of a book in itself, and their correspondence between 1909 and 1926 offers a wealth of insights. In these always cordial and genuinely respectful exchanges both men show interest, at least on the surface, in translating each other's works, but in practice this endeavour was barely consummated and was perhaps more of a token effort, an authentic desire lacking application. Perceptive to the work's credentials as an opulent contribution to early-twentieth-century literature rather than a vestige of nineteenth-century romanticism, Gide had published several pages of his own translation of the *Notebooks* in *La Nouvelle Revue française* in 1911. Rilke was thrilled and impressed with Gide's effort and returned the favour by translating the Frenchman's short story of 1907, 'Le Retour de l'enfant prodigue'. The act of literary translation always underscored the friendship and mutual respect between these two writers of stature. This collegiality extended into Rilke's early years at Muzot and beyond. Gide expressed a desire for Rilke and no other to translate his prose poem *Nourritures terrestres* from 1897, but Rilke was obliged to tactfully decline as he was then fully engaged with completing the *Duino Elegies* and could not afford to be distracted. Furthermore, he had the previous autumn started translating the poems of Paul Valéry. Though his letters to Gide allowed Rilke to develop his command of the French language, in the end his long-term correspondent was usurped by Valéry, who latterly won Rilke's devotion as a translator. It was in any case Gide's disinclination to return to *Malte* which paved the way for Betz.

The young Alsatian arrived at the apposite moment, and to Rilke appeared to possess the required sensitivity to bring his cherished prose work into the language he knew by now more intimately than any. Yet Rilke would not relinquish all control and would be very much present through the process as a guiding force, respectfully but firmly proffering his counsel.

The first, long-anticipated encounter between Rilke and Betz in Paris connects the warm correspondence to the collaborative work which proceeds during the spring months of 1925. The account of this first meeting is typical of so many of Betz's clear-eyed observations, which capture the complex subtleties of his revered subject's demeanour and only apply any mild criticism judicially. 'He approached me with outstretched hand, with an eagerness dictated by his natural politeness, but where a true joyfulness broke through…' One can't help but be reminded of a similar recollection of an enamoured Stefan Zweig meeting the Belgian poet Émile Verhaeren for the first time. The first impression of the other in the act of welcome appears to leave a powerful imprint on the psyche which resists deterioration over time. Betz lingers over Rilke's distinctive appearance and clothing:

> Rilke had this somewhat strange silhouette which I would become accustomed to seeing over the months that followed and which barely changed during his stay in Paris. He sported a grey felt hat, with round brim and flat base, light gaiters, suede gloves and a grey cloth overcoat…

Betz recalls that the two men quickly leave the lounge of the Foyot, where the presence of an English woman busy writing letters unsettles the ambiance. This passing remark, which could almost go unnoticed, is, in fact, revealing. For it sets the two men as an article and brings them together in their own conspiratorial entity; the outside world, represented by the English woman, perhaps a tourist writing letters home or postcards, is the Paris they wish to avoid. On the walk that follows down to the Seine they return by rue de Grenelle, a route which leads to a highly significant moment for Rilke. At no. 5 were the offices of the Gallimard publishing house, from whose basement Rilke, with Betz at his side, collects a box of his possessions and papers. These were the few things which Gide, through protracted and strenuous efforts, had managed to reclaim from Rilke's flat when Rilke, sojourning in Germany in the summer of 1914, was unable to return to Paris due to the outbreak of war. The loss of his possessions, abandoned in the flat at 14, rue Campagne-Première in Montparnasse, dealt a terrible blow. In Vienna Rilke had lamented his catastrophic loss to Stefan Zweig, who immediately galvanized his network of contacts to come to Rilke's aid. He contacted Romain Rolland, who in turn contacted Gide, still in Paris. Gide leapt into action but by then the bulk of Rilke's possessions had been auctioned off, having earlier been seized by the city authorities, who would have had few scruples when it came to the belongings of an enemy alien. However, he was able to procure from the concierge a box or two of Rilke's papers which had been overlooked. It was these precious documents and effects that Rilke was finally reacquainted with in the basement of the Gallimard offices.

Following the meeting at the Foyot, Rilke makes a preliminary visit to the apartment of Betz and his wife, and is enraptured by the romantic view of a still-bare, wintry Luxembourg from the fifth-floor balcony. Betz notes how Rilke clearly felt the attraction of being at a high vantage point, almost floating over the city, above the throng:

> He also liked that the apartment was separated from the street below by the balcony which ran along the entire façade, so that we could imagine ourselves raised aloft above the city, to a great height, as in a balloon basket, and that even leaving the windows open we enjoyed a feeling of isolation and intimacy.

On the next visit they get down to work. Each day, unless he happened to be ill-disposed through sickness, fatigue or some pressing obligation elsewhere, for he was much in demand, Rilke would arrive in Betz's apartment around 10 a.m. They would then spend a few hours together, sitting at either side of a small card table until lunchtime, poring over the manuscript of the *Notebooks* until it was time to carefully place the marker at a certain page and resume their labours the following day.

The relationship between Rilke and Betz is undeniably companionable, sympathetic, and their friendship clearly burgeons over these months of close proximity, enhanced perhaps by the strong element of trust and mutual accord necessary to achieve the translation. However, the work on *Malte* presents a considerable number of challenges due to Rilke's fastidiousness with a language of which he possesses the most extensive knowledge outside of his own. As Betz confesses here, offering what we must presume are only selective examples, Rilke is wont to pull his young translator up for not quite grasping the nuance or intention behind a certain phrase or image, by choosing a word which, though technically accurate or even artful, might give way to a more convincing alternative. These are the customary difficult choices for the translator, those necessary refinements which affect the long-term stability and endurance of a translation, but which are not always visible to the naked eye of the translator, however skilful. Betz treats the reader to a number of examples of these fiendishly tricky areas of debate, though due to the three-way language exchange of German, French and English, this is somewhat harder to follow in an English translation. (Please refer to the Notes.) Rilke more often highlights an issue, something he is uncomfortable with, then provides an alternative word or phrase which Betz almost always obediently accepts. Yet Rilke also offers praise for sections where he senses Betz has transmitted the rhythm and texture of the original with sympathy. Of course, it is very difficult for the layman to know to what extent Betz may have blundered or excelled, as we only have his word for it, and clearly he is not going to sully his reputation by his own hand. It is important to understand that Betz saw himself increasingly as the authorized translator of Rilke into French and, looking back, self-evidently wished to justify his first translation. His all but unbroken run of subsequent translations and generally accepted position as chief ambassador for Rilke in France is an endorsement of this covetous position.

But any Rilke/Betz symbiosis should not be romanticized; Rilke left behind an unpublished collection entitled 'Remarques à la suite de la traduction des Cahiers de M. L. Brigge', now in the archive of the Colmar public library, and it is from this extraordinarily detailed document that Betz sources most of the problems of translation he cites here. However, it has also been argued by critics and more recent translators of the *Notebooks* into French, perhaps more vociferously to condone the necessity of their new version, that Betz knowingly suppressed the most serious criticisms laid at his feet by Rilke in this document in order to justify his translation. Whatever the case, it seems unquestionable that Rilke genuinely believed Betz to be more than capable of undertaking the translation of the *Notebooks* based on a range of evidence, and doubtless a good measure of intuition. Rilke's respect for the translator who would conjure his work into the language he most admired was indisputable. But, any camaraderie aside, Rilke held to exacting standards and his knowledge not just of the historical subject matter, but also the subtleties of his images was always going to exceed that of the younger man. Anyone, however inspired, intuitive and skilful they might be, would, in my view as a translator myself, have had to bow to and benefit from Rilke's encroachment and augmentation. One thing we can be sure of is that the two men had forged a special bond by working together so intimately on the manuscript, for with no one else had Rilke worked so intensely and protractedly on his own writing. Betz, a young man in his twenties, had been permitted entry into a poetically complex interior world which few had witnessed at such close range, working at the rich seam itself, within the text, not only the mysterious sources and formations of the original being made manifest, but with the author of that text sat alongside him—verifying, endorsing, underlining, explaining, suggesting. Betz must have felt a tremendous responsibility and at the same time experienced a feeling of exclusivity in his privileged 'pioneering' position.

III

Whilst the evolution of the *Notebooks* in the productive alliance of its author and translator forms the core of the book, a plethora of other scenes in the life of Rilke, as recounted to Betz, both in Paris and at Muzot, have their place. Particularly intriguing for its cast of theatrical personalities and ensuing dramas is the period Rilke lodged at the Hôtel Biron, recommended by his wife Clara, to which Rodin was a late incumbent. The fiasco of the de Max affair, when the tenants were sent packing, is tellingly captured by Betz, who always keeps Rilke, the odd man out in such a milieu, in his lens, showing how the behaviour of these dandies and posturers impinged on his precarious unconventional existence.

> Rilke had as neighbours Jean Cocteau, the actor de Max and the Count of Osnowicine, who organized sometimes noisy nocturnal parties. One day de Max, who took great pleasure in sumptuous fantasies, had the idea of installing a bathroom in the sacristy of the disused chapel belonging to the Hôtel. This lit the touchpaper for a scandal which ultimately forced the administration to dismiss the most recently installed tenants of the Hôtel Biron.

Other memorable sections include the finely painted scene of a put-upon Rilke, during lunch at the Foyot, forced to answer the public telephone, since he refuses to have the intrusive device in his room, and being obliged to stand in a draughty hallway as cleaners pass and pairs of polished shoes are seized by unseen hands. The shivering poet, desperate to bring the conversation to a close, must endure the laborious and superfluous chat of a princess or countess stretched languidly on her divan, cosy and warm, before repairing to his room to find his lunch cold and the pages of the letter he was reading scattered over the table by a draught.

Betz includes the touching account in Chapter XIV of the renowned Italian actress Eleonora Duse, or 'Duse', as she was known, whose melancholy demise on an ill-advised tour across an America alien to her European sensibility affected Rilke deeply. Rilke captures the extraordinary sensitivity of Eleonora Duse in anecdotes recounted to Betz. These are scenes of tragi-comedy, where we witness the hyper-dramatic reactions of the actress to any infringement of peace, such as the raucous call of a peacock during a country outing or the buzzing of a fly in a friend's apartment. But whilst the rest chortled or sighed, Rilke knew that such responses were the result of her all-consuming inhabiting of the dramatic, that her temperament, her passion could expand boundlessly, that she was, in a sense, possessed. This total commitment to art reflected Rilke's own preoccupation and the dangers inherent when such a disposition collided with the rigours of earthly life.

Betz also excels in revealing how Rilke, especially during the Muzot period when he was saturated with solitude, both needed stimulating contact and yet quickly faded under the wearying demands of social connections. Betz compares the Rilke of 1925 with that of 1905, the one barely off the platform before he is besieged by those seeking his presence at some social event, the other stepping off the train into anonymity. Betz also touches on Rilke's arcane and uncanny presence at such society gatherings and the myriad, often negative reactions Rilke provokes amongst perplexed socialites and literary hangers-on faced with his enigmatic behaviour. Betz shows how Rilke's fragile health, his delicate equilibrium, could be adversely affected if any form of potential nourishment became too prolonged or oppressive. Even unbroken solitude, which he nominally sought, could prove corrosive, especially when combined with physical malaise. In 1926, following a monotonous round of treatments and periods of convalescence at the Val-Mont clinic above Montreux for an illness which was ultimately diagnosed as leukaemia, Rilke was increasingly determined, as his letters belie, and as Betz and others attest, to close up Muzot and spend the winter in Provence or Toulon.

Finally, Betz shows us a Rilke who when amongst friends and socially at ease tells wonderful stories, dishing out memories of his travels both moving and comedic; a Rilke who laughs cheerfully and like anyone else relishes good food and a fine wine. The scene of their celebratory meal together with Betz's wife to honour the publishing of the *Notebooks* is lovingly captured. This final section of the book also concerns the publishing of Rilke's French poems, the last poignant meetings between Rilke and Valéry at Thonon on Lake Geneva, the growing realization by some of Rilke's serious health condition, the initial hope when Gide, Edmond Jaloux, Pierre Jean Jouve and others are gathered in sombre attendance in the studio of Baladine Klossowska in Paris and learn from a telegram of his move back to Val-Mont. They erroneously interpret this as a positive sign, because on every other occasion their friend has left the clinic and returned to Muzot. Then later that month, Betz must ascend to Klossowska's studio again to receive the dread announcement. 'I just couldn't take it in; I still refused to accept it as I climbed the narrow staircase that led to the studio. I knock, the door opens. "*How is Rilke?*" He was dead.' Betz reveals his regret that he had never visited Rilke at Muzot, despite being invited on numerous occasions. It remains a mystery why Betz never made the pilgrimage so many others did, up the hill from Sierre train station to the hamlet of Veyras, thence Muzot, but he had to be content with a posthumous visit to Rilke's tomb at Raron churchyard instead and there maintain a silent vigil. Later, after learning of its state of neglect, Betz personally ensured the maintenance of Rilke's grave, and the planting of a rose bush to echo the now-legendary epitaph. *Rose, oh reiner Widerspruch, Lust, Niemandes Schlaf zu sein unter soviel Lidern.* (Rose, oh pure contradiction, desire, to be no one's sleep amongst so many lids.)

Twenty years later, in 1946, Maurice Betz, writer and translator, would himself die alone in a hotel room in Tours, quite unexpectedly. He was only forty-seven years old, four years younger than was Rilke on 29 December 1926.

Translator's Note

Maurice Betz wrote his memoirs of Rilke in his native tongue, French, but evidently he was obliged to quote from texts made by Rilke in German, such as excerpts from the famous 'Riding' lines of the *Cornet* at the start of the book. Though of course numerous examples in English exist, ditto the text of *Malte*, I felt it more consistent and uncluttered to offer up my own working version of these German samples to avoid any confusion and peppering the book with credits to various translators. Any French translation made by Betz from the German is then represented in an English version made by myself from the original.

Furthermore, Betz is discussing, predominantly in the important fifth chapter, the text of *Malte* and the challenges of translation, in this case suddenly drawn into the open by Rilke's criticism. Here I was obliged to don my mechanic's overalls and mount the English language as a complicating third wheel on to the French and German axle, to ensure that readers without those languages could have some conception of what was going on. This was an exercise which from the outset felt intrinsically precarious and liable to unravel into a spectacular abandonment of cogency and terrible disfigurement at any moment. However, by some miracle that did not occur, and the triumvirate trundled contentedly on. In practical terms, the solution was to include a note for each example, giving the possible English meaning of the word of the German and/or its French equivalent as chosen by Betz or later suggested by Rilke as an alternative.

Readers with some knowledge of the languages involved will necessarily be in a position to travel more deeply into this terrain, but those with English alone will at least be able to define features within the panorama. Naturally, any failures in this regard may be gleefully placed by wiseacre critics at my door, though forgive me if I do not open it.

ON THE DISCOVERY
OF RILKE

NEUCHÂTEL, 1915. How can so many days of such clarity and depth melt away without leaving the slightest trace? All then seemed new to our eyes. Events proceeded with a spirited and perilous mobility. Things owed their meaning not to themselves but to the scent of the season, the colour of the air, the suggestion of a lake, to a thought from the sky. In a headlong rush we devoured Taine, Renan, Barrès, and the news of a certain war which was already making itself heard across the world. But of what importance Taine or Renan, what of Verdun or the Marne against the contented crackling of a fire of pine logs in the hearth of a chalet lost in the combes of Chaumont, or beside the puerile pleasure taken by a few friends in ransacking the liqueur trove of some resigned parent, or beside a nocturnal walk at the close of afternoon beneath the trees lining the quay, between the lake of silver and the old château shaken by a passing tram crammed with schoolchildren and young girls?

To be frank, we were seventeen. To us Rousseau seemed an older brother whom we addressed on first-name terms and to whom we were now making a pilgrimage, crossing over to St Peter's Island[1] upon a flower-bedecked boat filled with young girls and students in velvet berets. We set out in the depths of

1

night on the most marvellous and surreal walks, searching out a reflection of ourselves, in the damp orchards of Saint-Blaise, in the gorges of the Areuse or on some lane winding through the vineyards.

Some mornings our youth weighed less than a desire. In the evening, on occasion, Marcel Hofer—who was yet to be named Lucien Marsaux and had not then written either the *Prodigues* or *Le Carnaval des vendanges*[2]—drew me into his room, whose windows, open to the breath of the Föhn, looked over the port, to read me lines such as these:

> Oh hazy weather, sky of grey,
> tree that a breath has barely disturbed,
> innocent sweetness where time invites you,
> oh hazy weather, sky of grey.
> Quiet afternoon,
> the schoolchildren's song, oh lost steps
> below the paths where coming joyfulness
> gleams in the meek branches...

Unless it was this little poem to which a part of our youth clung:

> To the festival clear and pure
> Where no women appeared,
> The white clouds alone were
> (carried on a weak wind),
> invited by spring.

It was on an afternoon in that ageless season, perhaps a rainy day, certainly a spring day, that I was paying a visit to an old Alsatian friend, indulgent to our youth to the extent of fostering our vague literary curiosities: Professor Schneegans. The library of this scholarly specialist in literature of the Middle Ages included not only the classic texts of the *Bibliotheca Romanica*,[3] to which he guides us with such intelligence, but still the best authors of the *Mercure de France*[4] and *La Nouvelle Revue française*.[5] Taking advantage of the permission he had granted, I would go over from time to time and draw from its shelves a Claudel, a Francis Jammes, an André Gide or a Remy de Gourmont.

By what stroke of fate could it be that a slight cardboard chapbook, its German title printed in gothic script, found itself that day squeezed between two volumes which carried as watermark the Symbolist caduceus? As if the significance of that discovery I was about to make, without realizing it, had gifted me in that moment with the power to record more clearly, I see with utmost precision the study lined with books, the shelf I explored that day, the reflection that emanated from the glass door of the corridor, and even now I can sense at my fingertips how the rib felt protruding from the solid spine of that little volume.

Then I remember nothing, except that, beneath the green and white cover, flowering like a design from a tapestry, this little book bore a strange title: *Chant de l'amour et de la mort du Cornette Christoph Rilke*.[6] I took it, along with a Laforgue or a Suarès, only opening it a few weeks later.

In which of the furnished apartments which we had successively occupied in this Swiss city (moving on to a more stable set-up, awaiting the end of the war which we persisted in believing was imminent) did I read this poem by Rainer Maria Rilke for the first time? Was it avenue du Premier-Mars, where our neighbour was an elderly, virtually deaf German professor who introduced his students to Sophocles and Euripides, raising his voice (which he himself barely heard any more) to declaim these verses from

Sophocles' *Antigone*—'Shaft of the sun, fairest light of all that have dawned on Thebes of the seven gates, you have shone forth at last, eye of golden day, advancing over Dirce's streams!' Or perhaps it was at the corner of rue du Musée, where from my window I would sometimes spy J.-H. Rosny aîné[7] strolling along the lake with his distracted faun-like face shaded by a beard? I no longer remember. But I know that when finally, one evening, I opened this little book, the distant ride of Cornet Christoph Rilke across the plains of Hungary suddenly seemed more real to me than the war which shook Europe to its core:

Riding, riding, riding, through the day, through the night, through the day…
   Ride, ride, ride.

And courage is so wearied and the longing remains so great. There are no mountains now, barely even a tree. Nothing dares to stand up. Strange huts squat thirstily near marshy wells. Not a tower anywhere. Always the same view. You have two eyes too many. Only at night sometimes you imagine you know the way. Perhaps at night we always return to the piece of land we laboriously won under a foreign sun? That may be. The sun is heavy here, as at home in mid-summer. But it was summertime when we said our farewells. The dresses of the women shone for a long while out of the green. And it's so long we have been riding. It must be autumn. At least yonder the sorrowful women know us…

So there was this strange country where young soldiers withered like flowers on their velvet saddles, then came to life breathing a rose or recollecting a song. Between the fires of the bivouacs beat the heart of a world that we had always sensed and whose existence was finally revealed to us. Horses were carried away, music was lost in a park, there was wine, there was blood. There were also clouds, as in the sky of our own springtime, and the night sometimes leant over these images, fresh as a woman. Yes it was a dream, but it was more: life, more real, more disturbing than we could have ever imagined. And someone had seen these shimmering figures pass over clouds, one evening, in his room, someone, a poet, perhaps a young man, who had that somewhat strange name which we heard for the first time: Rainer Maria Rilke.

I read this book in one sitting and Marcel Hofer read it after me. Then, very rapidly, other works by Rilke began to surround it on my desk. These were *The Book of Images*, *The Book of Hours*, *New Poems*...

As long as one is young, one is capable of an enthusiasm so powerful, so absolute, that one can make room in one's life for a writer even knowing barely anything about him. Ignorant of Rilke himself, we indulged in his poetry with an even greater appetite. Had we known that one day he would pass by this lake and a few years later in those nearby mountains come to die,[8] it would have moved us no doubt, but we would not have loved him any the greater. More than from any of the sources on which we had been nourished until then, it seemed to us that we were feeling in these pages the very presence of poetry. Our life was changed.

We knew already that poetry is only created out of clear ideas, happy assemblages of words or rhymes, assonances and feelings. But these verses taught us much more: a way of naming things and, through them, to penetrate into ourselves, a means to participate in life, in what is most impressive within it, most mysterious, most poignant, a state of passionate and painful contemplation, an exaltation that raised us out of ourselves. This was poetry; it was the experience of all this, become blood, glance, gesture and transmitted in the subtlest ways. This was a poet. His image, like a circle on a pond, could in our eyes widen without needing to be clarified...

When I happen to reopen these books that I've never been able to separate entirely from the landscape of pines, the lake in summer, the umbelliferous herbs in the wind, of youth and pastures, where I welcomed them for the first time, I find on their endpapers dates and places such as 'Neuchâtel, 1916', 'Lugano 1916', 'Lausanne 1917' and in one of them—a small German edition of *The Notebooks of Malte Laurids Brigge*[9] with green covers where I had inscribed hastily in pencil: 'January 1916'—I read a little further down this dedication which Rilke, having ten years later found the volume on my table in Paris, had there inscribed in his beautiful and restful handwriting:

To Maurice Betz, confirmed through the prolonged and active possession of this book which he acquired better than any other. With all friendly gratitude. R.M. Rilke. Paris, in June 1925.

I

THE BOOK OF IMAGES,
CIVILIZATION, 500,000 SHELLS

THE FOLLOWING SPRING, Marcel Hofer, who was a few years older than me, was doing his military service in the Swiss army. Beneath the dark-blue uniform of an artilleryman, he went on manoeuvres upon the slopes of the Dent de Morcles, bearing baskets of shells beneath the branches of larches.

One morning he returned in haste to Neuchâtel for twenty-four hours' leave to spend a last day with me, because now it was my turn to wear a uniform. I had signed up at the French consulate in Bern, a voluntary commitment, and I was summoned to the recruitment office at Besançon to receive my assignment there. One last time we spent a long evening together and only bade our farewells after midnight. At six o'clock in the morning Marcel Hofer was at my door again, fitted out as an artilleryman. Before rejoining his regiment, he wanted to accompany me to the station, where we going to be parted for a long time.

But during the months which had preceded this re-encounter and farewell, we had still enjoyed in Neuchâtel a drawn-out winter of purest friendship. 'A winter', Marcel Hofer had written somewhere, with many sleepless nights in the shadow of the church, with many grey days beside the green lake, smoking and reading Rilke and Léon-Paul Fargue, with all the daydreaming at the university and toiling away on the benches, for in February we had metamorphosed into actors and we'd been applauded or whistled at in Neuchâtel or Couvet, in the Val de Travers, in the Chaux de Fonds, all over, in the larger mountain villages where the snow and the firs celebrate their splendid nuptials...

Amongst the two or three volumes that I packed in my baggage as a future French soldier was a collection by the German-language poet Rilke. This volume, *The Book of Images*,[1] rested for a long while on a plankboard of kit in the old arsenal of Cherbourg, lately transformed into a barracks and which resounded with the kicking of freshly landed Canadian horses; we gazed at it over long nights in the guardhouse of I don't remember what little Norman station, lit by a wood fire where we roasted cider apples; it fell prey to damp at the Mailly camp, was spattered with mud at Montsuzain, then for a long time was bumped about in a dark-red haversack carried by a train of soldiers on leave, with a horde of men, unkempt, drunk, wild with joy, from Châlons-sur-Marne to Paris and from Paris to Angoulême. Finally, one morning, it made its appearance at the front, between Dormans and Château-Thierry, where my battery, as if in a last effort to delude itself, had taken up position in a still-verdurous corner which went by the charming name of Fleury-la-Rivière...

But I shall refrain from recalling all the peregrinations of this little book, fortunately provided with a hard-wearing cloth binding. Many times it seemed as if its destiny was to be separated from me, as on that evening when we hastily evacuated a position after being spotted by the enemy and to which I had to return to find my bag, forgotten in the shelter. On other occasions I was tempted to unburden myself of this extra weight, and when I slipped it into the bag of a favoured comrade, whose baggage was travelling on the top of a wood-sided wagon, it left me for some time, without being lost entirely from view, and from the summit of its observatory, swaying to the slow cadence of the horses, it was obliged to witness many fantastic landscapes illuminated by the glimmer of shells.

In the notebook which always accompanied me I used to jot down half-melancholy, half-ironic notations, like this brief *communiqué* in which Rilke's book took on a virtue of exorcism:

> Live, only live…
> My dugout is a walnut shell on the side of a volcano.
> At any moment the lava can flow over us
> I feel like laughing or crying—I don't know any more.
> Laughs, friends, travels, green mint…
> The shells are strident and gleeful.
> The echo sends them back to me from the valley depths
> and to defend myself I have
> a gas mask, a Spanish model revolver,
> a flash of sunlight on a wall and *The Book of Images* by Rilke.

In those days, what were we reading to fill the hours of forced recreation? Some took great delight in the film of Clément Vautel, and there was *Le Canard enchaîné*,[2] which only providential cyclists sometimes brought into our desert haunted by hyperite gases. As for the articles of Maurice Barrès,[3] they seemed to us a nonsense, a fatal aberration. Everything that exalted our disgust and sought to gloss over our wretchedness with delicate, shiny sequins could only appear to us an offence, and if it has taken me a long time to return to the enchanter of my first sixteen years, it's only because of the resentment that his *Chronique de la Grande Guerre*[4] left in me.

What singular power over souls would have been necessary to persuade these half-deranged men that there could still be somewhere other than these holes, this maternal earth, this rain, and from time to time the heat of *eau-de-vie* in the belly. A vehement forced gaiety could sometimes deliver us from our terrors, and more rarely the echo of an almost forgotten verse, like the blows struck against a wall which let the buried miner know that all hope for rescue is not lost.

Around August 1918, after zigzags across zones of armies, the meaning of which remained as baffling to us as to a rabbit in its burrow the planetary system—our column emerged one morning in one of those rare landscapes where the war had revealed itself.

The guns had rolled on all night; we had crossed woods by paths where one became stuck in the mud; we had waited for hours at the edge of a road for orders which never arrived; we had dashed across dangerous crossroads and a bridge harried by enemy artillery; we had passed through ruined villages where the darkness was thicker (save for a few veiled lights at the air vents and red dots of cigarettes); we had climbed up impossible steep slopes clinging to the wheels of our guns. We went on piercing the dark night like a worm in wood—from time to time, the dented silhouette of a covered wagon, like some exotic beast of burden, lit by the flashes of shooting—and suddenly we were overlooking a vast plain where the war appeared before our eyes in the pale dawn, as if we had taken a shortcut.

In the distance, a dull rumble, as of a cart pushed over uneven cobbles, announced that the offensive was close. The road had just formed a curve and this is what we found. Five kilometres of moving rucks stretching as far as the eye could see, a single slowly moving snake lacking head or tail. Now and then in the grey or brown, black or russet patchwork an absurd flame burst forth above which rose white smoke.

An ammunition depot, camouflaged in green and yellow, appearing like an impeccably laid out French garden. At most the shimmer of a heap of copper casings here and there betrayed the immoderate taste of the owner for those white and yellow balls that decorate suburban gardens. Five hundred thousand shells of all calibres covered the garden with a homogenous and priceless humus. Every day it was nourished by three or four trains, though it never seemed saturated, for all the roads heading north exhausted it unremittingly, and at nightfall fifty batteries scattered in the surrounding woods spat their flames.

A river was cast across the plain like a bar of lead. Towards evening, the sun lit everything and hundreds of horses trudged to the watering hole. Trampled by so many hooves, beaten by shells, the pastures were further discoloured by tarpaulins. A dead horse was smoking, spreading a nauseating stench of burnt horn and rot. Somewhere a tree raised its black stump into the bare sky, the murky night gradually drew in around it, but this only lasted a few moments. Barely had darkness fallen than the war rekindled on the horizon a bloody dawn...

I had taken advantage of our last rest, before this stage of unexpected length, to bathe in a river. It left me in a bad way since, during this interminable walk, my heavy boots cruelly wounded my feet softened by the water, so I was obliged when we arrived at our new position to find a doctor to dress them. In the ambulance, which had just pulled up nearby and whose staff had in expectation of the coming battle a good deal many graver concerns than welcoming a limping artilleryman, I was received rather brusquely.

However, I ended up by finding a young auxiliary doctor who agreed to take care of me, whilst rebuffing me out of habit when he spied, in the pocket of my jacket, the reseda covers of a delivery of the *Mercure de France*. It had come in a parcel a few days earlier along with a tin of conserves and the ubiquitous pair of socks. And I had read there, under the pseudonym of Denis Thévenin, behind which Georges Duhamel concealed himself, one of the most beautiful pages of war penned by that writer.

'What? The *Mercure* here? And you have time to waste! And might we know what in there so interests you?'

I told him about the chapter on civilization I had just read and he smiled at my enthusiasm. But the professional ice was broken. In the disorder of this flying ambulance, we chatted for several minutes of things terribly distant. Of things to which my interlocuter was much less of a stranger than he strove to appear, for the names of Baudelaire, of Rilke rose successively to our lips. I left him finally with a breath of confidence, carrying away a few morsels of advice on the best way to conserve my feet in case of further forced marches.

———

The great offensive of August 1918 was triggered a few days later, and I never saw the young auxiliary doctor again, that friend of poetry with whom I had spoken then, in the woods of Fère-en-Tardenois, of Baudelaire, Rilke and also the early wartime prose of Georges Duhamel. Later I imagined that I had met Duhamel himself, but, following the knowledge of the author of *Salavin*,[5] I convinced myself I was in error. Towards the end of the month, in spite of everything, I ended up losing *The Book of Images* that had faithfully accompanied me on so many paths, those muddy expanses of the Aisne and Marne. On the other hand, I was loaded down with two American tent sheets, several cans of solidified alcohol and other utensils of more immediate utility.

The offensive brought us close to the station of Fismes, in a mineral water depot abandoned by the Germans but where we still received their shells. Here we lived for some days in an abundance of carbonated, digestive or diuretic waters produced by the German soil. In these surrounds I happened to find at the bottom of a German shelter a collection of Bismarck's letters and a war novel by Ernst von Wolzogen[6] in a popular edition. It was this volume which served as a replacement in my haversack for the Rilke. I held on to it for a long time because of the name of the German owner, written on the flyleaf, which made me dream (I had also found in the book the photograph of a woman and fragments of letters), and I was trying to imagine his thoughts, lying in my shelter, on this mouldy straw where my turn had come to be devoured by lice saturated with German blood. However, I never managed to advance beyond the first few chapters of this novel. As soon as I was able, I bought a new copy of *The Book of Images*.

II

DADA, MALRAUX, COCTEAU, HARDEN

THE DISCOVERY OF RILKE at seventeen, the war at eighteen, Paris and the most marvellous peace at the dawn of the twentieth year... when I look back on it, it seems to me that these experiences succeeded each other in this particular way as if to be in a position to instil in that which followed a more solemn and truthful resonance.

Now Paris was welcoming us, filled with its processions, its victory parades, and offered us the unknown quivering of its pleasures and thoughts. Despite the brilliance of those ardent years, the most powerful memory I possess of this time is a sense of malaise, a terrible feeling of emptiness and sterility; after having lived so forcefully and so alone with ourselves, after having dreamt of expressing our cruel or blissful conquests, we were seized with an invincible disgust for any action, whatever it might be, even by the act of writing. Our keenest visions dissipated, our questioning lost its impetus. Artifices were our dreams, our hopes, beneath this gaze of the dead we could never forget.

We had walked there in a light which had blinded us for so long. In this horrible drought we amicably embraced the worst days of

Rimbaud. We were violent, ironic, contemptuous and unyielding. The pride of our misfortune rendered us yet more unfortunate. You could have said that all that was youthful in us, for having steeped ourselves in this adventure, had suddenly turned against all life, against humanity and against ourselves.

We discovered something of this belligerence and this need for negation in the cynicism of some writers of our own age or who were a few years younger than us. Marcel Hofer had joined me in Paris, and with a sympathetic curiosity we were attending the early Dada performances in the Gaveau room, where Louis Aragon, a pink cherub like a soft bonbon, struck blows at the heavens and strove in vain to conjure his own charms.

Doubtless we guessed that he was adopting a demeanour of youthful impertinence and naive taste in these violent entreaties, which at least were only verbal. However, it was their very excess which led to a rejuvenation in us. And we were already caught up in the game again when he happened to repeat such a melodious verse to us:

The dream where you bit into watermelon interrupted…

'Why are you writing?' then enquired the literary review of its collaborators. 'I am touched that you are waiting for my reasons. But ultimately I write little.'

'Your reproach scarcely touches me,' came the rather slapdash reply of Jean Paulhan.

Well we didn't write much either. One day, though, Marcel Hofer undertook a great Claudelian[1] dramatic work which he sent to Jacques Copeau at the Théâtre du Vieux Colombier, where an admirable interpretation of *The Winter's Tale* had enchanted us. The manuscript was returned to him accompanied by a polite refusal. Even if the play had been of a higher quality it would still have met the same fate, because in his creative fever Marcel Hofer had changed the name of his hero no fewer than three times and he had entirely forgotten to make the necessary corrections to the manuscript, in such a way that in the second act Folletête changed into Noirmont and became no less explicably Gaydamour, or something like, in the third act.

A little later, Marcel Hofer redeemed this failure and he was able to announce to me triumphantly that he had just found a publisher for his poems. Months passed, the publisher went bankrupt and Marcel Hofer left for Germany and Austria. Taken over by a creditor, the publishing house was once again threatened with liquidation. The volume by Hofer finally appeared in conditions so idiosyncratic that I am probably the only person to own a copy, and these verses from Lucien Marsaux's youth can be considered as almost new:

> Leap from behind the western mountain
> towards the east, borne on this fresh wind,
> clouds of damp spring,
> who will wash ashore on woods I know,
> blueing with a happy shadow the road long followed
> and the inn, the inn where we drank that wine,
> (a wine such as we will never drink again)
> You can crown the leafless branches,
> you so white and bushy and pure as then,
> but I hate you, clouds,
> clouds of this spring.

In my turn, I gathered together a few sheets, crumbs of war tobacco, which had remained deep in my pockets and my satchel, and I took this manuscript, which I had called *Scaferlati for the Troops*,[2] to a backroom on the Quai Saint-Michel where the portrait in the window of Verlaine had drawn me and where an honest shopkeeper, as M. Jourdain would have said, sold prose and poetry that he only distinguished by way of the printers' costs. 'No doubt it is far too late to bring her up again', I had written in the form of an epigraph on the first page of the pamphlet, for it was 1921 and the war seemed to us then an event almost as ancient as the Flood.

But what chance for my young war tobacco to find a few smokers? One morning the postman delivered to my student room one of those letters which, for a youthful unknown poet, will eternally prevail over the strongest rewards of life.

Florent Fels,[3] André Malraux and Georges Gabory then published the review *Action*,[4] in which Blaise Cendrars, Max Jacob, Jean Cocteau, André Suarès, André Salmon, Francis Carco and others collaborated. Its first success was the seizure of a number containing a eulogy by Landru, whom the Versailles Court of Assizes had just sentenced to death.[5] Alexis Danan, who had not yet taken up the reporter's pen, contributed prose poems. Jean Cassou, himself waiting to encounter on his path the poet of the *Duino Elegies*,[6] celebrated darkness there. Vlaminck's woodcuts illustrated these texts, alongside the last *calligrammes* of Apollinaire. Marcel Sauvage was to proclaim in *Action* that a new poet had just come into being, and the letter announcing this event invited me to I no longer know which table in the venerable Rotonde.[7] The publisher of *Action* was the Stock bookstore, which a few months later published my first Rilke translation.

Action, when I became acquainted with its directors and where I was invited to collaborate, suffered the fate of most fledgling reviews at that time and of all times: having passed the milestone of the first year, it never appeared again. In its place we saw a literary collection spring up in small-format editions at a modest price, *Les Contemporains*, which, at a time when weeklies had not yet been born and when advertising had no place in the world of letters, seemed to us the antechamber of literary glory.

In this collection, which he directed from Stock, Florent Fels published texts by more or less consecrated authors, presented with sometimes severe prefaces by young writers who seized an opportunity to affirm their tastes. Marcel Arland drew a portrait of Henri de Régnier, whom he greeted with a condescension verging on the ironic, as a 'beautiful example'. Jean Giraudoux rubbed shoulders with André Gide, the Tharaud brothers, Georges Duhamel, Edmond Jaloux, Pierre Mac Orlan and Jean Cocteau.

Florent Fels's office was a small, rectangular room on the first floor of the Stock bookshop, almost always invaded by piles of new editions, where one met on certain days of the week more artists than writers. We would take lunch at the Petite Chaise or Vendanges de Bourgogne with André Malraux, Salmon, Créixams or Mac Orlan. Malraux, who was talking about his forthcoming departure for Indochina, whilst waiting to experience *Les Conquérants*,[8] dazzled us with his peremptory judgements, his competence with the stock market, the facility of his speech and the perfect cut of his suit. Receiving these compliments, he replied: 'There's nothing to it, I am always dressed by the first tailor in Paris.'

Pierre Mac Orlan, with his curious eyes, that brush of hair on his forehead, was writing *Malice*.[9] Jean Cocteau in a light suit was already young, as young as he would always remain. He was the only one amongst us who had come close to Rilke, but he had barely been aware of it himself. At the Hôtel Biron, before the war, he had been Rilke's neighbour,[10] and Rilke told me later how he had often 'attended' parties from his window that Max and Cocteau had organized in the park of the boulevard des Invalides.

> Long, long after, [wrote Cocteau in his *Portraits-souvenir*,][11] I had to know whose lamp it was that surveyed every night behind a corner window. It was the lamp of Rodin's secretary, M. Rilke. I thought I knew a lot of things and I lived in the crass ignorance of my pretentious youth. Success deceived me and I didn't realize that there was a kind of success that was worse than failure, a kind of failure worth all the successes in the world. And I was also aware that the distant friendship of R.M. Rilke would one day console me for having seen his lamp shine without understanding and how it beckoned me to go and burn my wings there.

Raymond Radiguet was another of ours, one evening, in a bistro in the faubourg Saint-Martin, that had unearthed Fels. I remember him as a large, silent boy, with thick brown eyebrows, with the softness of suede, above wild and watchful eyes.

Marcel Arland customarily showed himself only rarely, but on occasion he would come to Fels's office to smoke more and more English cigarettes, a game, explained it seemed by the presence of a secretary, blonde or brunette, to whose charms the young author of *Terres étrangères*[12] did not appear insensitive. One day a fairly lively altercation ensued between Fels and Arland.

The next day, on my way up, I met on the stairway two witnesses of Arland's who had come to challenge Fels to a duel and whom he had just shown the door without the least form of due process, by using the familiar *tu* as usual. The matter must have been settled later and without bloodshed on a terrace of Les Deux Magots, as I heard no more about it.

If this incident has lodged in my memory, it's probably due to the fact that it was the same day that Fels had asked me to suggest some texts by German authors for the collection and, if necessary, to translate them. Since he had just devoted pamphlets to Jaurès and Charles Maurras, his desire was to begin by welcoming a political author.

We talked about Maximilian Harden, whose *Die Zukunft* had ceased to appear, but about which there had just been countless questions following the Grunewald attack which had almost cost the life of the famous polemicist.[13]

Fels wanted to publish in the style of the great German pamphleteer a portrait of Stinnes, or Rathenau, and he asked me to carry out the necessary research on the collection of the *Zukunft*. That same day I named other German writers and offered to translate a fragment of *The Notebooks of Malte Laurids Brigge* for *Les Contemporains*, a major work by a German poet completely unknown in France, one Rainer Maria Rilke.

Having some idea of the *Zukunft*, I was accustomed to the dense style of Maximilian Harden, all those intertwined sentences, sewn with snares, incidentals, parentheses—and as a novice translator, I did not approach this work without apprehension. Harden wrote to me:

> I don't need to tell you that everything depends on the quality of the translation. And it's not because I doubt your skill that I kindly ask you to communicate to me the trials you undergo, but to enable me to possibly dissipate any misunderstandings (always possible), and to complete my text with the opportune additions that the moment might suggest to me.

In fact, the translator on whom Harden bestowed such confidence had under his belt no more than a few high school versions, and so he was obliged to apply himself rigorously so as not to disappoint the author of *Sexagesima*. I displeased him though, if not by my translation then by my preface which at the request of Fels I had written for this little book. Having become easily piqued with age, Harden was in fact irritated by what I myself thought I should have indicated, if only out of concern for the documentary facts, that his real name was Witkowski. He held fast to the notion that there was an antisemitic slur on my part, complained to the publisher and our relations came to an abrupt halt. However, with Harden's *Stinnes* having appeared, I reminded Fels of our project to make room for Rilke in *Les Contemporains* and encouraged him to read some fragments of the *Notebooks*. The wonderful passages about houses being demolished, that hallucinated Paris of walks and meetings with the young Dane, conquered him immediately, and Jacques Chardonne, co-director of the Stock house, was also visibly struck by the acute and uncanny sensibility betrayed by this work.

As luck would have it, I had just found, whilst walking the *quais*, an old issue of the *La Nouvelle Revue française* which, to my surprise, informed me that André Gide had already translated a few pages of the same book a dozen years earlier. His translation had appeared at the same time as an essay on Rilke from the pen of Mme Mayrisch de Saint-Hubert.[14] This precedent and the authority of Gide helped me to overcome the editor's vacillation. Now all that was left for me to do was to inform the author of my project and obtain his approval.

III

FIRST LETTERS FROM MUZOT

WITHOUT KNOWING RILKE AT ALL, I had the feeling that he would not entrust the task of translating his *Malte* to the first unknown who set eyes on it, and that in his view a translation must be the result of a considered choice, the culmination perhaps of a long frequentation, the fruit, in any case, of a particular affinity of taste and thought.

In order to furnish him with at least one element of appreciation, I thought to attach to my proposal letter for the project the sole book I had published at that point, this *Scaferlati for the Troops*, which I have only mentioned earlier with some insistence because it pertains to the first letter I received from the poet. In the secret hope of tempting Rilke, if possible, I enclosed with my package the exquisite little volume of Colette which had just come out in the collection of *Les Contemporains* under the title *Rêverie de nouvel an*.

One day in January 1923, two envelopes, one containing a letter and the other printed matter, departed separately, both bearing the address of the publisher Insel in Leipzig, to whom I entrusted the care of passing them on to the recipient. On the first page of my little book I had traced in German the sentence by which Malte Laurids Brigge, after formulating his exacting conception of true poetry, judges and condemns his own verses: 'All my verses originated another way, so there are none.'

Barely a week had passed when I received in a blue envelope sealed with a red stamp a registered letter from Switzerland. On the reverse it bore mention of the sender: *R.M. Rilke, Château de Muzot-sur-Sierre, Valais, Suisse.*

These words, along with my address, were written in a neat script, slightly slanted, quite high, somewhat feminine, where the capital Ms were inscribed with a certain momentum and where the R was embellished everywhere with the same step at the top and the same hook at the base of the letter.

How many I have received since of these letters, which appeared identical from the outside but each containing a particular message, some new and unique. Sometimes the colour of the wax or seal would change: from red the cachet became grey and the effigy faintly enlarged of those arms which one day Rilke would announce to me in heraldic language. Between sable and silver, two greyhounds rampant opposite each other.

But the writing remained the same until the end, with the exception of a few notes drawn up in Paris where one senses the haste, and save for the final letter I received from him, a few weeks before his death, where the script is broader and leaning, as if weighed down by the burden of suffering. Characteristically, these letters, like all those Rilke wrote, spoke a language precisely matched to the recipient. Despite some preciousness of form, and I know not what affectation of style from the employ of a foreign language, they succeeded in touching with deepest sensibility our personal relations and, like dehiscent fruits, opened when the moment came to deliver up their delicate flesh.

Already that first letter which Rilke wrote to me bore an instant and direct accent:

What my young Dane claims to know about verse, is of his own experience:

Let us not mix everything up. Inevitably there are thousands of ways to forge it, from your poetry, and yours, born of a pure enthusiasm, filled with such simple obedience to this sublime impulse, deserves without fail to be esteemed and loved. What I have done: 'One evening, (before the hearth) / In the countryside…'

Even if I don't count some touching surprise prepared for me on page 53, [Rilke was here referring to the little poem 'Communiqué', collected in *Scaferlati for the Troops*, and where I had mentioned his name without suspecting that one day he would read this book] *I have, it seems to me, particular reasons to welcome these intimately rhythmic words whose calm brings transparency to the emotion from which they came. Already during my first reading yesterday, I paused at many a line…*

Thank you for your kind attention; I regret having nothing at this moment to better answer it. That will be for later.

Under the registered envelope which contained this letter I had, to my surprise, discovered the Colette chapbook that I had sent along with my own. I would receive an explanation for this later: my letter had not reached him.

Unknown to you the chapbook must have somehow slipped into your own volume that I have just received. I hasten to return it to you, resisting the temptation to cut out the pages and read it before you… (But taking advantage of chance luck I shall ask my bookseller for a copy.)

I quickly cleared up this misunderstanding, and in a fresh letter, supposing the first misplaced, I once more informed Rilke of the project which explained my double mail. The answer was not long in coming. Rilke wrote to me on 20th January:

So I had not only the right to keep Colette's little book, but to see there a precursory sample of an achievement which would be dear to me above all others!

Really, you wish to dedicate yourself to this translation and include a fragment of The Notebooks of Malte Laurids Brigge *in that interesting collection* Les Contemporains? *But I am so touched!*

Knowing nothing yet of your kind intentions, I told you, in my first letter, the sympathy I bore towards your book; so no need to insist on assuring you that it is with perfect confidence that I accede to your project of labour. May this work cause you more pleasure than fatigue.

This book, which could only have been written in Paris (where I lived for almost twelve years and where I learnt almost everything required to create it), already had the signal honour to attract the attentions of André Gide. You are probably too young to remember the pages, incomparably translated by him and so close to the original that they made my heart miss a beat. (Published in the N.R.F. *in 1913 or 1914, I am not sure).*

I add—herewith—a brief note for your publisher which I ask you to pass on to him.

Your two letters took it upon themselves to arrive here together in the same mail; each completed with a few strokes the image of your warm interest, to which responds, believe me, my sincerest sympathy and deepest gratitude.

―――

I had undertaken the translation of the *Notebooks* even before receiving this letter, and fifteen days later I was ready to bear my manuscript to the Stock bookshop. Rilke, who was in no way disinterested in my work, despite the confidence he had expressed in me with such delicate courtesy, had requested of Fels to have a copy of the manuscript and the proofs.

On 19th February he shared with me his impressions and some criticisms in the following letter:

Dear Sir and poet, by this same post I have returned to Monsieur Fels the manuscript he kindly wished to lend me: I read it with a particular attention and with increasing satisfaction; for it seemed to me that your hand, page by page, becomes freer whilst moving closer to the cadence of my text. On occasion we recognize some difficulties, surmounted moreover with taste and courage,—in short: everything combines to render your valiant effort sensitive and profoundly moving to me.

If I include some remarks, please accept them as mere propositions; you will have time to employ them during the correction of proofs.

It remains for me to fill out a little the dates in your introduction.

I was born in Prague on 4th December 1875. I spent my childhood and part of my adolescence there. I completed my studies in Prague, Munich and Berlin. The greater part of the years 1899 and 1900 I spent in Russia (the decisive event of my life).[1] *In 1902 I came to settle in Paris, which I never left (until July 1914),*[2] *other than to make further trips, a great number, in Italy, the Scandinavian countries and in turns Algeria, Tunisia, Egypt and lastly Spain, where I thought to stay for a time.*

Enough. I never read what is written about my work and I loathe talking about myself, save to a few friends or lady friends… and only very rarely. Be assured, dear sir, the sentiments of my sincerest sympathy.
R.M. Rilke

After the translator had completed his labours in less than a month, the publisher and printer showed somewhat less urgency. It was only in mid-July that the little volume of *Les Contemporains* appeared which contained, beneath its straw-yellow cover, the title in prominent capitals along with a brief notice on Rilke, about a hundred pages of *The Notebooks of Malte Laurids Brigge*.

A few days later the pamphlet was in Muzot, in Rilke's hands, and I received this letter from him dated 25th July 1923:

Dear Sir, on Sunday I completed my reading of our little volume of Les Contemporains. *For me there was an indescribable emotion in seeing these returned pages and in some sense, instead of their origin, now identified with the intimate conditions which gave birth to them.*

If—four years ago—the Danish translation managed to touch me by making a little less authentic my semi-imaginary character, I recognize him more now since you have set him back in his environment, verified and controlled by this return of language.

I cannot conceal the fact that the emotion I experienced reading your translation could never have reached such potency nor such an even continuity, if the precision inherent to the work had been less; for it seems to me that you have endowed your French version with a measure of that obedience which I once employed to form the original.

I congratulate you, dear Sir, on the result of your faithful efforts; I very much hope that you are not left without some agreeable echoes as recompense for your modest and protracted labour; in the meantime, know that my most vigorous gratitude keeps you company...

From that moment, I had expressed to Rilke my intention to continue the translation of his work, with a view to publishing it in its entirety. The remainder of this letter alludes to this project:

If now I express the desire to follow on the continuation of your work, do not suspect me of yielding to distrust. It would be a sincere pleasure for me to collaborate with you over the few suggestions which, at a certain point, might perhaps facilitate and simplify your task. So then, do make use of me.

To apply some more sensible weight to the balance of my gratitude, I graft to these lines a little book of Sonnets which has just seen the light of day; perhaps it will arrive in good time to accompany you on your holiday.

On the subject of holidays. I recall that some of your poems are dated from the 'Val d'Illiez'. In spite of my geography, which is more than wanting, this Valaisan name inspires me with the vague hope of seeing you ascend one day to my equally Valaisan venerable château. I shall end there by bidding you welcome, once and for all time. Yours affectionately, R.M. Rilke.

I did not take up this invitation literally, despite its warm-hearted simplicity, and in any case I was committed to spend that summer in a farmhouse in the Vosges, in the company of a dog, a sparrow-hawk and the manuscript of my first novel, which was slowly being sketched out.[3] *The Sonnets to Orpheus*—for this was the work which Rilke had sent me, a precious copy on Japanese paper, as a pledge of his gratitude—doubtless accompanied me there, but I fear I was not at that time of the mind to access their translucid beauty.

Facing a grey-green ravine, at whose foot lurked the village of Labaroche, under the old thatched roof I lived for more than six months, amongst the firs and pastures lit up on occasion by the lightning of a stream, I would doubtless have felt more comfortable with those first French verses that Rilke was to send me the following year in an issue of *Commerce*:[4] this sleeping woman that I too had below my gaze as I wrote, this nod to chance and to the seed that germinates, and, mingled with the sound of cowbells, this futile call to the springs that surrounded us on all sides:

> water that hurries on, that runs,—forgetful water
> that the distracted earth drinks,
> hesitates a brief moment in the hollow of my hand,
> remember!

IV

PARIS, THE FRENCH LANGUAGE, BERG AM IRCHEL

Neither this year nor the following did I go to see Rilke in Muzot, although he had renewed his invitation on a number of occasions. And in fact it was he who, quite unexpectedly some eighteen months later, came to us, lured by friendships and Parisian memories whose call had resounded within him and became ever more pressing.

This attraction that Paris and France exerted on Rilke and the publication of the French translation of the *Notebooks* had perhaps combined to render even more forceful that pull which he had always experienced. In August 1902, his first sojourn, he settled in a hotel room in the Latin Quarter, and those initial letters betray his emotion and the strength of feelings which swept over him. '*I'm in Paris… I am one in waiting: what will I become?*' He writes to Clara Rilke. His first visits are to the Louvre, Notre-Dame, to Rodin, the Cluny Museum… '*Reading books, taking notes, thinking, calm, loneliness: everything I was longing for.*' But soon he comes to realize: this city is dense, '*walled up in odours and breaths*', '*heavy and anguished as if beneath ground*'. After the vastness of Russian life he penetrates into another immensity, made up of faces, sounds, memories, monuments, works of art, of men...

Joyful men who laugh, full of exuberance, serious, sad, silent and lonely men, men of all kinds, today, yesterday and tomorrow...

At the outset, this city appeared almost hostile to him, and never had a nostalgia for Russia overtaken him with so much force. But little by little he discovers the city's beauties, her hidden corners, her parks, her sources of solitude, her secret gardens, the marvellous accords of her skies and light. After only a fortnight he laments his inability to grasp the language, so he 'invents' his first verses in French and sends them to Rodin with the following words:

Sometimes I feel the spirit of the French language, and one evening, walking in the Jardin du Luxembourg, I created the following verses which are not translated from German and which came to me on who knows which hidden path...

Adding that it was his admiration for Rodin[1] which had inspired him and that: '*It is the desire to draw closer to you which guides my hand.*'

From his first stuttering confidences to Auguste Rodin right up to his admirable letters to Baladine Klossowska,[2] Rilke never stopped using French whenever the individual correspondent or the need of the moment prompted him to do so; and it seems we must seek the origin of Rilke's French poetry, at the same time as the increasingly in-depth knowledge acquired by translating Gide and Valéry, in this custom of corresponding in French, which year on year had more urgently imposed itself on him.

When his confidences, always personal, rise in tone, when he feels the need to communicate to a male or female friend some fleeting emotion that seized him at a particular moment, the letter tends to quite naturally close with a poem, or is accompanied by a few verses for which he more often than not excuses the insufficiency by confessing to the 'spontaneous dictation' from which he suffered. And, recommending a certain indulgence of his correspondent with these songs from his 'little lyre', Rilke professes to be pleased that this passing wave did not carry him further away.

To Lou Salomé,[3] who before the war had worried about seeing her friend helping himself so frequently and so willingly to a foreign language, expressing the fear that the poet was in danger of losing his intimacy with the German language, Rilke replied:

Oh! No, on the contrary, this intimacy augments it! Think then of the infinite number of words that I spare for later, by not wearing them out and rendering them banal through daily use.

But this temptation nevertheless concealed pitfalls which Rilke could not evade. This foreign language, which he claimed to make use of in order to spare his own, also possessed its privileged words, its singular turns of phrase, its unrivalled beauties. Already, in a letter from 1907, Rilke confessed to the Swedish writer Ernst Norlind,[4] whom, moreover, he had counselled elsewhere to beware of the temptation to write in a foreign language, that sometimes he used French to say certain things that would have been simply impossible to express in another language. André Gide, in a diary entry dated January 1914, showed precisely how Rilke encountered some shortcomings of the German tongue: fully occupied translating Michelangelo's *Sonnets* and seeking an exact equivalent for *palma*, the poet translator noticed that German had a word for the back of the hand but none to designate its interior. As if to attenuate his infidelity to his first language, there is a similar discovery alluded to by Rilke in the writing of the word *verger* on the cover of his first collection of French poetry:

> *Maybe if I dared write to you,*
> *in borrowed language, it was to use*
> *this rustic name whose sole empire*
> *always tormented me: Verger...*
> *Verger: Oh privilege of a lyre*
> *to be able to name you simply;*
> *matchless name that attracts bees,*
> *name that breathes and attends...*

By inserting this new word and a reality which, by its impairment, might have escaped him, Rilke shows quite clearly that he was not simply obeying an artist's temptation, but the fortuitous desire to inaugurate a new means of expression. Jean and Jérôme Tharaud[5] reported in their memoirs of Maurice Barrès the disdain that their friend demonstrated towards foreign languages:

> A writer [said Barrès] receives no benefit whatsoever knowing any language other than his own... foreign languages have only served to say the same nonsense in two or three different ways.

A wisecrack which perhaps explains the strange poverty of interpretations concerning the people and German characters that Barrès put forward in his work. For Rilke, on the contrary, language, in its properly poetic conception, is being, and each language contains the essence of the people for whom it is the means of expression. It's not only to know Tolstoy or Dostoyevsky better that he spent long months learning Russian, to confirm through '*This great and grand certitude that Russia is my homeland.*'

Rilke also had quite the opposite experience: he told me one day that he learnt English in a few months so that he could read Keats and Browning. But, disappointed by these poets, he experienced such a sudden distancing from England and the English language that he almost as quickly forgot all he had just assimilated. He came to the view that England stood outside the enchanted circle of his experiences and the possibilities of his nature. Thus his memory summarily rejected all that it had once welcomed, as if it had never been.

It is a fact which one cannot fail to be struck by, that the oldest of Rilke's French poems—if one neglects his rare and less complex essays of the pre-war period—is dated 'Munich 1918', which perhaps allows us to locate during the last months of the war the moment when Rilke was, for the first time, overcome by a feeling of nostalgia for the France from which he had been absent since June 1914.

A letter to one Frau von Mutius reveals that he was preoccupied with the mystery of languages and already secretly attracted by the French language, though already well aware of the essential dangers. To this correspondent, who, in the midst of the war, had offered up to him a number of French translations of his poems, he wrote:

PARIS, THE FRENCH LANGUAGE, BERG AM IRCHEL

What profound joy, what power to entrust to a language so conscious and sure of itself a lived sensation, and to ensure that it introduces it in some sense to the domain of a general humanity.

It has often seemed to me that one who writes in French may be required to work against the current of the foreign tongue, for it is almost the stronger when one enters into the struggle with it; entering it completely means to submit to it, but with what superiority and what sovereignty is it not recompensed by this benevolent collaboration? It makes academic, if I dare express myself in this way, the contribution imprinting its mark and poured into it and thus lends it the aspect of a noble thing understood.

The German word in its poetic ascent has a tendency to evade common understanding and must be caught up by it one way or another. Even more so the Russian word, which is perhaps a mere shred, a kind of banderole in one's hands. And owing to the fact that over there each human being is literally in search of the other, it is transmitted like a contagion, blood to blood.

I was tempted seventeen years ago, in Russia, to appropriate it as a language, as the most consistent for my state of mind, even for my poetic work. It goes without saying that this would have entailed enormous losses; we should, fundamentally, write in all languages, so that this feeling of being without a homeland, of which you most justly complain, might also be proclaimed joyfully like the awareness of being a part of the 'great All'. Since childhood, my heart and my spirit have been oriented towards this idea of a patriotism which is universal and of a global equality, a conviction from which I cannot distance myself even today, so you will understand then how much I suffer...

―――

After his cruel war experiences, Rilke began by temporarily accepting the hospitality of Princess von Thurn und Taxis in Venice, where the recollection of old memories barely appeased him; then he roamed for a time through Switzerland, not yet knowing if he would settle there permanently. Basel, Geneva, Nyon, Locarno in turn welcomed him, but did not wholly satisfy. He lamented that nothing properly touched him any more, that, since the 'wretched disguise of the uniform', the wind, the trees, the stars had somehow become foreign to him. His anxiety was aggravated by the vague yearning to find inspiration for the *Elegies* he had begun to write in 1911, in Duino, and from which the war had separated him as if by an abyss. It was at this time that a desire arose in him to return to Paris and that a stay there might eject him from this torpor and show him the path that would take him back to a liberating past. He left suddenly, without letting anyone know, and remained there for six days, in complete solitude.

Of this first stay in Paris, following the war, I only know what Rilke told me of it four years later and what we can glean from the rare letters in which he declaimed his joy. He had wanted to see no one, had informed no friend of his visit. Moreover, two of those closest to him had died towards the end of the war and he would never see them again: Rodin and Verhaeren. So sudden had been his decision to leave that he did not even enquire about the box of papers and books he had been obliged to abandon in his apartment in June 1914, and of which Gide only managed to save a part.[6] He came alone and in an unknown hotel sought to be a stranger, like the young man who had settled in the furnished room in the rue Toullier,[7] and had lived there in Paris for an apprenticeship or as one recovers from an illness. Immediately on arrival he had taken to walking, following streets at random, as in former times.

Anguish of this first contact, an attempt so filled with risks. It was like trying to kindle a perished love, which before the war had already been slipping away.

Lou Andreas-Salomé affirms that in 1913, Rilke, suffering a phase of weariness, had fled Paris, and even she had failed to persuade him to return. And in a letter to Princess von Thurn und Taxis he complained that, following a walk at Versailles, everything felt '*worn out, worn out for me*'. '*I don't even care any more for these admirable ragpickers of Paris.*' As if this '*admirable*' somehow seems off-key in such a confession, and which furthermore belies the remainder of the letter:

> *Only the minor events still sit well with me, such as this cat I observed yesterday on boulevard Montparnasse: a leaf was falling (there are some falling), the cat began playing with it, then sat, coquettishly waiting, watching over the tree with its round, green gaze, for when it launched other leaves, poised to play with them, with autumn itself.*

When Rilke found himself in Paris at the end of October 1920, he did not immediately feel liberated. Strolling any which way, he had traversed part of his old *quartier* and arrived somewhere near the rue de Seine and the rue Bonaparte, in that network of lanes which extend between the boulevard Saint-Germain and the Institut de France. Suddenly he espied in front of one of those antique shops that he described in the *Notebooks*, their windows filled with curious trinkets, a cat whose tail seemed to brush along the spines of the old books and whose owner sat at his table, spectacles perched on his nose. He recognized the window, he recognized the brooches, the snuff boxes, the ivories, the enamels laid out there and he saw that the bookseller had not changed in the slightest. Lifting his gaze, he suddenly recognized the very tie the old man was wearing: a black and red check, fixed with a gold clasp. Rilke told me:

At that moment, a keen, forceful sensation of joy overcame me. If all this had stayed the same, even the antique dealer's tie and even that horseshoe pin of metal that I recalled, then anything could begin again, then I too must have remained the same. I had found my old Paris, my eternal Paris... I had no need to converse with anyone to convince myself of this. The streets, the gardens, the quays, the Louvre, the very sky itself spoke a language clearer and more consoling than any other. I departed a few days later, satisfied, enlivened by a great courage and renewed confidence.

Rilke returned to Switzerland, where his friends, however, had actively expressed their concern for him. Barely had he arrived when another of his wishes was fulfilled: they had put at his disposal a small castle near Zurich, quiet, isolated and at the end of a large park, which would be all his until the following summer.

On 16th November he expressed his profound relief in this letter whose communication I owe to the addressee, Mademoiselle Elisabeth von Schmidt-Pauli,[8] who, understanding the value of such testimony, entrusted it to me, requesting that I publish it as a message to Rilke's French friends.

Château of Berg am Irchel (canton Zurich). 16th November 1920.

Dear Sister Elisabeth, it's not the work, no, it's a persistent insecurity, one which appears incurable, that has rendered me incorrigibly uncommunicative on all sides; thus even your good and confident news has remained unanswered. 'I'll be with you soon,' I kept wanting to write, and yet I knew that I would not come as long as the slightest possibility remained for me to stay in Switzerland, to stay once more in Switzerland. And here

I truly remain—all is resolved—and I even found the power of speech (at least for a moment).

Dear Sister and friend, just look at this little image, the château of Berg am Irchel (it's not a river, this Irchel, but rather a hill, in the background of the park). Look at it well and bless it for me. This will be my winter: to live as a solitary here, cared for by 'Leni', the governess who (just between us) has considerable qualities Rosa lacks, for example she does not take my taciturnity to heart and accepts all plainly like an objective attribute that one may note without further interpretation.

Leni is therefore my sole companion at the château of Berg, I've been here three days and already things have taken on a regularity, my God, how much I needed this! Blessed is he who does not date his desires; here has come to pass what I so ardently wished for when I arrived in Switzerland, and what I had first hoped to find in Nyon, at the Countess Dobrenzsky,[9] and last winter in Locarno; then it was still somehow forced, but here it presented itself freely, without effort, and it was perfectly ready, with its fountain before the quiet windows, this strong and ancient old stone house whose gables (like so many other things in Switzerland) remind me of Sweden.

But what use this favour of silence if I hadn't experienced Paris beforehand? Yes, imagine, I have seen it again and from the first it was possible for me to live in the most assured continuation. Ah! As my heart is applied to the bad wounds of the past, it has adapted everywhere precisely, healed! That it could overcome! It was only then that I knew how much I depended entirely on this resumption of contact with the world at the very place where... it became world for me, unity in itself and transition towards me. Now I have experienced it, with what profound simplicity and what happy serenity, and it is only by being aware of this that I can hope to continue.

And your winter, Sister Elisabeth? Where are you? What becomes of you? In what field are you currently active? Administer well my American fortune, it's not the only thing that grows under your dear and faithful guardianship. Send my regards to your family (The Schaumburgs, 'Madi') and all the common friends who 'survived' with you. Awaiting news, your Rainer Rilke.

'*I like it when the circle closes, when one thing joins up with another,*' said Rilke one day to Edmond Jaloux, alluding to his journey through Spain, which had confirmed in him old presentiments and where he had recognized certain images from his dreams.

But the circle could close in many different ways. Returning to Venice after the war, Rilke had only experienced a sense of terror. As he wrote later to Lou Andreas-Salomé,

My desire to find everything unchanged, as unchanged as possible, was accomplished so literally that we were always on the verge of living, beyond the unutterable years, that simple repletion, the 'one more time', which was made possible in the most distressing manner, because we were forever approaching the circumstances in relation to their resemblance; but the heart, whose arrest during those years of war due to its supreme vitality was also to remain unchanged, equally welcomed in the same state those identical things of former times; and then shattered this sentiment of 'nothing but repetition' that almost overwhelmed me with terror when foreseeing it from afar...

From whence does it come, this terror which dogged Rilke in Venice, so much so that it put him to flight, but which in Paris enchanted him to such an extent that he felt attached by an indissoluble bond and was drawn there ever more irresistibly?

V

ÉMILE-PAUL, JALOUX, BENVENISTE

THE HISTORY OF THE RECEPTION accorded a work of art by a defined public in itself offers only anecdotal interest, secondary at best. Too many chances and misunderstandings enter into the frame, inevitably. Especially a work like that of Rilke, one so deeply personal, demands to be considered above this murky mélange of salon conversations, chatter about authors, fashions and prejudices, where judgements are formed and where, in France at least, the reputations of writers are established.

The work of art, as Rilke said, requires time and silence.

However, the reception given to his work in France must have touched Rilke in particular ways. If he persisted in his willingness to ignore criticism, if, until the end of his life, he only approached certain tributes with infinite caution, as if they might be an explosive material, he was not nevertheless insensitive to personal testimonies which found their way to him, whenever they bore a sign of genuine sincerity, outside of literature. It was letters, calls, confidences which brought him closer to his imaginary hero and which connected him by new threads to this Parisian climate in which he had immersed himself for a few days and of which he had begun dreaming again in his mountainous retreat.

In a letter he wrote to me later he qualified this '*ambassador close to you*', this Malte of whom he loved to talk like a mutual friend, as a witness to our conversations or a familiar host. The young Danish hero was in truth Rilke's ambassador to all his French readers, and this envoy sent on many reports of the affections he had aroused.

I know that the very humble form of the little printed notebook on rough paper by which Malte had addressed the French public had pleased Rilke no end. No doubt, later, when we came to a consensus at rue de l'Abbaye with Émile-Paul[1] and Edmond Jaloux on the presentation of the complete edition of the *Notebooks*, and it was decided that this work, which in German comprised two small volumes, would be combined into one larger volume for the French edition, Rilke, feigning a childish joy, exclaimed:

What good fortune! I, who always dreamt of having a 'spine' and who until now had to make do with only chapbooks. So finally we will have, Malte and I, our 'spine' where his full name can appear. Providing that this dear friend does not get ideas above his station!

But in the meantime, it delighted Rilke to appear beneath the quite simple exterior of this little volume which had the appearance of a popular edition. The spirit of the book's presentation formed a bridge with the memory of those first Parisian years when he had felt irresistibly drawn to the lower strata of the city and when he had led an almost destitute existence.

If he loved that a poem stood out harmoniously on the blank page, if he possessed an almost sacred respect for the manuscript, the tangible form of the work, he did not share the bibliophile's appetite nor the craving of a collector. On the contrary, he was seduced by the notion of being able to slip this small volume into a pocket, take it to the countryside or to a public garden, leafing through it whilst walking, and that strangers who had no knowledge of his name could happen upon it by chance…

This little notebook was a perfect match for the first of Malte's Parisian experiences whose experiences were the backbone of this incomplete edition. Rilke only stipulated one condition. He wrote to his publisher: '*I desire a pure and perfect iconographic absence.*'

Furthermore, the portrait which was to accompany the work was deleted at his request during the printing.

This discreet little notebook caused a resonance far beyond what one might expect from its modest dimensions. Perhaps its appearance was of the moment. I am not sure if ten years later it would have aroused such immediate interest. Without a doubt, the name of André Gide significantly helped draw attention to this unknown German poet. Be that as it may, the success the work enjoyed was of an exceptional magnitude and velocity.

Edmond Jaloux was one of the first to discuss it in his *Nouvelles littéraires* series.[2] He said that the *Notebooks* represented 'the notes and meditations of a character who not even Dostoyevsky could have sired'. 'In a fortuitous montage, the author furnishes us with his daydreams, his memories, his anxieties, his joys, his observations, his hopes. We already have many books of this genre, but then these are perhaps the ones to which we return most readily…'.

Later he admitted that 'this more or less secret element of the personal that such a work suggests' was for him the special attraction to the *Notebooks*. 'For me, as soon as I had read *The Notebooks of Malte Laurids Brigge*, I experienced an overwhelming desire to meet Rainer Maria Rilke.'

Pierre Mac Orlan, who then ran a literary column in *La Petite Gironde*,[3] also admired this writer of rare sensitivity, who revealed such profound originality in his reactions to both real and imaginary life: 'Those who have read this little book will have taken a further step on the road that leads our sensibility towards who knows what intelligence, which day by day becomes ever more provoked.' Others, like Félix Bertaux, in the *Nouvelle Revue française*, placed himself at a greater distance: 'The scent of these shed petals evokes the past, summons the fever of 1903.'

But it was above all in the reviews of the youth which came into being and then passed away, so numerous since the end of the war, that Rilke found a rapt audience. I have conserved amongst others an article that appeared in the review *Philosophies*, run by Pierre Morhange,[4] where Émile Benveniste defines in joyful terms the spell of Rilke's prose:

> Baffled at the beginning, and to break the prestige of such an invocation, we should like to arm the analysis with the virtue of an exorcism. But we must change our instruments: our criticism has barely only studied dense or diffuse works, those always fixed or that it served to fix. Now we need to invent a more dynamic criticism which will adjust to notations as tenuous as those of Rilke, one which can follow in its double and thwarted game the action of the forces which dissociate this curious personality: a multifaceted and submissive sensitivity, capable of fusing itself into the very heart of things, and a gift of total recapture, acute, by way of an intelligence which remains ever vigilant. That sensitivity which first penetrates the

most intimate recesses of beings until it identifies with them, retracting with a jolt.

Rilke lives therefore under the sign of terror: anxiety is the place for sensitivities that cannot comprehend. Hence this whispering voice, this poorly repressed trembling. Why this mask that conceals being? Or does a being not hide behind the mask of things? This is the dilemma which tears into him and gives rise to his anxieties. But this terror is not seized and articulated at the moment of the crisis, it is rather incorporated into incidents of the most mundane life, it circulates there like a potion with a protracted progression. And when chance presents itself, barely muted or already dissociated, the contradictory forces out of which we attempt to reduce the conflict, Rilke himself is his chosen subject: in this he proves an equal to Dostoyevsky, as in those pages which describe the divine torment of an epileptic who with unclouded vision senses the approach of a crisis.

A moment later, the world has restored its empire; no more choices nor weariness: an invasion of images that cling, an agglutinative receptivity, if I may say, words relinquish all meaning; all boundaries are abolished, beings freeze or float, things come alive and take on the most bizarre relationships: 'The street was empty. Its void fell prey to boredom, drew my step out from under my feet and played with it like castanets on either side of the street, as with a clog.' And all this, painting or reverie, memories or meditations, is evoked by words which always renew the suggestion, in a prose forever traversed by mysterious correspondences.

I felt I should report this article to Rilke and attached it to one of my letters, but he never departed from his commitment to a principled silence. He returned it to me shortly thereafter, without allusion to its content, thanking me with a simple courtesy.

Rilke, provisionally, therefore remained foreign to this movement of sympathy that the *Notebooks* provoked. If he participated at all, it was largely through personal letters he received and to which he responded with a tireless conscience. The arrival of a bouquet of flowers touched him far more than any newspaper article, a letter from a woman more than a writer's praise. He was invited to Pontigny, but he declined at the last moment. What would the poet of the *Elegies* have been doing in this rustic academy of philosophers?[5]

But apart from these direct appeals and personal relationships, Rilke felt equally attracted to France through the books of this post-war generation whose notable names had surrounded him in this small *Contemporains* collection. He confided to Countess Nora Purtscher Wydenbruck:[6]

So many beautiful and enchanting things have come to me from Paris, it is quite astonishing to see so many fine and noteworthy books produced by the young and the youngest French generation. I have the highest hope that the regard of these young men (there are a great many testimonies in this sense) seem to become more and more equitable and attentive concerning foreign and external things, without the least of the world denying itself.

And in a letter to Mme Gertrud Ouckama Knoop:[7]

I can't tell you of all the wonders that France bestows on me; I am surrounded by them. With all I have at my disposal I devote myself to the purchase of books which are now being born there; for so many of them are such that one should not only read them, but often reopen them.

Now the boundaries have really fallen away there. The French spirit, becoming aware of itself with a new vitality, no long in fear of welcoming things foreign and distant... And the influences which we thought had passed by before the war (or that we would have misunderstood, by locating their spirit) seem already assimilated in the purest way in the works of the younger generation, those for whom the war has been something of a puberty of heroism.

However, I continued to send him requests which reached me and which, through the translator, were addressed to him. Edmond Jaloux, who didn't meet him personally until later, wanted to publish new fragments of the *Notebooks* in *La Revue européenne*.[8] Robert de Traz requested a text for *La Revue de Genève*.[9] The belated response which Rilke afforded me dismissed these requests with the same gesture of courteous and rather weary indifference. From the sanatorium Schöneck, in Beckenried on the shores of Lake Lucerne,[10] he wrote to me on 1st September 1923:

Dear Sir, the need to undergo a fatiguing cure allowed me to be distracted from the most agreeable duty, namely of informing you how I felt and how much once again I appreciated the sympathy demonstrated by your good letter. It's this same fatigue (the healthy kind, I hope) which obliges me to be brief today.

I already knew your dispositions towards me—you have provided beautiful and fine proof and you continue in that vein. But you really surprised me, summoning the precious interest which was to be found with M. de Traz and Edmond Jaloux (reading the latter is always a profound pleasure and highly rewarding experience for me).

My commitments with the Stock publishing house are of scant detail. In my view I can see no impediment to there being publication in review of selected parts of your new translation. However, to avoid any confusion, you might do well to secure the consent of the editors, at the pertinent moment.

Please accept, my dear Sir, my best wishes for your work, that which concerns me so intimately and the others,—and please know, affectionately to you, R.M. Rilke.

Concerns of another kind had distracted me from my work, and it was only a few months later—after Robert de Traz had brought it up again—that I managed to send Rilke a first part of the remainder of my translation.

From Muzot he acknowledged receipt of it to me, on 7th March 1924, through the following letter:

My dear Monsieur Betz, if I saw it coming, last evening—with much pleasure on the back of your translation, I can however assure you that I was expecting it without impatience; for I am too partial to slowness in everything which concerns the work of art to permit me such a feeling; I almost blame Monsieur de Traz for having imposed this haste upon you.

I will do my utmost, however, to give him the manuscript as swiftly as possible. I am counting on Sunday to devote myself to close reading, which—I have no doubt whatsoever—will confirm the keen acknowledgement that I bear you.

I have been told a lot of good things about your Alsacien novel;[11] *also I am delighted at the thought of reading it over the summer during those few months which I consider to be those of vacation. Presently I am working, not as intensely as I would like, often being interrupted by my health which is rather shaky this winter: but I work.*

One of your compatriots, my friend M. Jean Strohl (professor at the University of Zurich), has long since instructed me to express his sympathies to you; if you ever come to Switzerland, he will be at your disposal; he is a charming man who devotes himself to matters of the spirit with an admirable deference.

And if ever such a trip comes true for you, do not forget how much we expect you at Muzot. Be assured of my grateful good wishes. Your R.M. Rilke.

A week later, this letter informed me of his impressions after reading:

Château de Muzot-sur-Sierre, Valais. This 7th March 1924.

My dear Monsieur Betz, since Sunday I have immersed myself in your manuscript, and the result... the result is that I beg you to devote—with all haste aside—a few more hours to revise it, guided by the remarks that I should like to add to it.

Do not be alarmed if you find them in great number; I preferred to share with you all my concerns, and I have arranged things in such a way as to make it easier for you to verify as much as possible. I know that you are too determined to do well, to fear that such precaution would seem pointless.

You allowed me to introduce into the text some changes which seem necessary to me; I employ this freedom for the simplest cases. But for everything else, I can only offer you my notes as proposals; I have too much respect for your work to insert myself there by force, and the danger would be too great of disrupting with intrusive words the intimate rhythm, so essential to this kind of prose, which you were able to grasp with incomparable attention. Some chapters, such as the description of the Cluny museum's tapestries, lose all value if we cannot successfully reproduce the deeply interior melody of their development.

If difficulties accumulate in the first pages of your manuscript, the fault lies with my text which, in passages that evoke Beethoven or the dramatic force of Ibsen, moves further away from Latin thought and of all the equivalents that could be found in the language which excel in making this thought vital and clear. There you were forced to struggle in abstractions.

So once again, dear Sir and collaborator, I am entrusted to your care… leaving you all the time to reflect and compare. I also think I know why we rushed you a little from Geneva; it's because I was invited to give a conference there, and no doubt Monsieur de Traz would have wanted this fragment to be published around the same time. Unfortunately, due to my inclement health I could not apply myself to it, and I suppose that—the conference being postponed—the Revue de Genève *will not be in such a hurry to receive your manuscript. And besides, after looking over it again, you will send it directly to Geneva, now! Kindest regards to you, R.M. Rilke*

P.S. Please excuse the disorder of my notes, so caught up in the reading as I was and I don't really want to read through it again, to not linger longer… a potential snag occurs to me: will the printer cope if we load more on to the manuscript, already complicated enough in places? Should we perhaps have a clean copy made? R.M.R.

Rilke's remarks on my translation were traced in black ink on around twenty large sheets of squared paper, paginated in blue pencil, and where the references to pages on my manuscript, as well as certain observations of general character, had been made, for greater clearness, in red ink.

The clarity of this manuscript, the meticulousness of these precautions contrasted with the rather shapeless rough draft that I had abruptly decided to send to Rilke, renouncing any further development of a text which could have been extended to infinity and promising myself, at the sight of my crossed-through manuscript, to return to it, following an annoying custom—on the proofs.

These sheets that Rilke sent me contained the summary of a certain number of obvious errors of interpretation, doubts expressed about the precise meaning of this or that word, and a good number of questions which he left to me to answer:

Could the word *inouï* be used in French in its etymological, literal meaning? Hadn't it been too blunted by its use in the figurative sense, and would it not be preferable to use a periphrasis to induce the difference that the German language makes between the words *unerhört* and *ungehört*?[12]

From a passage which related to Ibsen and which I translated literally as 'because you had in your blood to reveal', Rilke proposed a freer but more assured version: 'because it was the power of your blood to reveal'. And he added:

This passage is not yet completely clear; it wants to express that Ibsen made the decision to enlarge what he observed in his test tubes, so that some fact or some change, minuscule before his eyes, appeared enormously magnified in his dramas, from now on, visible to all!

Elsewhere, on the contrary, Rilke maintained his own text, warned against deviations which could lead to error. I wrongly translated *cadenette* as *fourragère*.[13] Rilke observed:

However, I find in the Larousse: 'Cadenette', n. f. Long braid of hair falling on each side of the face, which certain corps of troops wore…' This was exactly what Christian IV wore: why wouldn't we then retain 'Cadenette'?

The questions followed one after another, countless: was it necessary to translate *unbeirrbar* as *immuable* or *imperturbable*?[14]

Would such a case be better rendered by *puis* or *alors?* Had I checked the wording in heraldic language of arms? Was it sufficient to say that this mourning dress was *effacée*? Couldn't we, in order not to lose the idea of silence which was contained in *verschwiegen*, to say of this dress that it was *muette*?[15]

Rarely was Rilke tripped up by any insufficiencies in his practice of French. Thus, in a sentence where is used the expression *n'avoir de cesse que*, he enquired, with logic on his side:

Isn't the word 'quand' missing after the 'que'? Should we not write: 'Ils n'avaient de cesse que quand...'?[16]

Question marks in red ink punctuated a doubt, or underlined a hesitation that had come to him on second thought; and lest I should be scared off by many of the problems he posed to me, he had sown here and there, again in red ink, some praise: '*Page 6: a very beautiful page, really successful,*' or '*Pages 14 and following, the story of the dog Cavalier wonderfully rendered!*'

This letter, these criticisms from Rilke were for me a lesson which is not the only one I owe to his lofty example. They immediately made me think of the sentence from the *Notebooks* on Félix Arvers:[17] '*he was a poet and he loathed approximations*'. They showed me that, if he knew how to welcome generous dictation from his unconscious, he also knew how to apply the long patience of the craftsman, having learnt from Rodin that love and nostalgia for beauty are of little use if, thanks to the hard labour, we do not first prepare the conditions capable of allowing them to be embodied in words or things. And above all it seemed to me that I was only at the first stage of my enterprise, that the greatest challenges of my translation, revealed as a preliminary draft, were still lying in wait for me.

The summer was spent on this work, resumed, interrupted, the job restarted...

It was almost with regret that I sent Rilke my first novel, which I had already wanted to see destroyed. I reread the *Sonnets to Orpheus*, for which I had barely thanked him the previous summer and whose solemn beauties had only now begun to appear for me.

A trip to Rome was planned, but then postponed... There was no question of going to Muzot. At the end of August I received the following letter:

Château de Muzot-sur-Sierre (Valais) Switzerland. This 26th August 1924.

My dear Monsieur Betz, the people of the Valais have been surprised by their cool and rainy summer, so at odds with those summers we are accustomed to here; I am (from my tower, my garden and my little vineyard) Valaisan enough to be amazed with them, but that aside I have other reasons for astonishment, though these belong particularly to me.

My summer is going quite differently to how I had foreseen: I saw myself as the great reader in the shadow of my two trees, and now I find to the contrary that I have been almost always absent from Muzot, only returning from time to time to give myself a fright when faced with the piles of mail that have amassed during these various absences! Behind the hills of these letters I can make out these lovely books that I desire to read; but I can't manage it—save for this Parrot-green beauty of Princess Bibesco[18] *that I brought back from my travels, they're not even cut yet.*

So may this explain my silence to you! I am so ashamed of not having thanked you for your book (I always intended to do so after my reading of it)—and that I was able to accept without breathing a word in response to your long and fine letter, and later this notebook of Tendances[19] *that I explored with keenest interest.*

I was still counting on your trip to Rome, with the selfish notion that I would be indebted to it for your visit to Sierre. But it didn't come to pass. If I don't stay wholly occupied with work and fall short of my intentions there, it may be that I shall pass a few weeks in Paris this autumn; in such a scenario, one of my first undertakings will be to come and shake your hand. At last!

Sincerely to you! R.M. Rilke

For the first time Rilke announced to me his next arrival in Paris. His project was realized a little later than he then foresaw, in January 1925.

VI

LES CAHIERS DU MOIS, STERNHEIM, VALÉRY

FOR ABOUT HALF A YEAR I had been taking a more or less active part in the writing of *Les Cahiers du mois*[1] which André and François Berge had founded in 1923 and which published works by the likes of Marcel Arland, Sherwood Anderson, André Beucler, Emmanuel Bove, Louis Martin-Chauffier, César Santelli, Carl Sternheim, as well as critical issues and documentaries.

Like many youthful magazines of this time, *Les Cahiers du mois* was not wholly convinced of its own inner necessity; it was rather a field of experiences, a somewhat obscure terrain which extended from Massis to Gide, Bergson to Keyserling, and where the surrealist Philippe Soupault rubbed shoulders with Raymond Régamey, already prepared to don the white robes of the Dominicans. This eclecticism, which was the leitmotif of *Les Cahiers du mois* and which allowed Marcel Arland, amongst others, to group together in an examination of conscience diverse and moving testimonies on the generation which was dubbed *la génération du mal du siècle*,[2] was not without certain disadvantages. With a curious and wide-ranging intelligence, François Berge infinitely broadened the framework of each *Cahier*, and to ensure that no point of view was neglected, not only solicited all contributions, but went so far as to never refuse any that were submitted. It followed that the *Cahiers* kept expanding. But because we couldn't increase the print runs and price to the same extent, it meant death in the short term.

However, the *Cahiers du mois* survived for two more years. Their name sometimes led them to be compared to the *Cahiers de la quinzaine* of Péguy,[3] which at least assured them a degree of honour. Having on two or three occasions supported the rather superfluous necessity of selection, they awarded me the title of editor-in-chief. I took advantage of it to suggest some preferences and compose some issues, including *Reconnaissance à Rilke*, which appeared in 1926.[4]

———

At the end of 1924, I had translated for *Les Cahiers du mois* a short story by Carl Sternheim, which appeared at the same time as a number of columns on German letters. Naturally I had requested permission from the author of *Europa*.[5] Great was my surprise when one day André Berge told me that he had just received a letter from Sternheim, who, having arrived for a few days in Paris, said he had seen a copy of the French translation of *Busekow*[6] in a bookseller's window and protested against a publication he claimed to be entirely unaware of.

I decided to pay a visit to Carl Sternheim to clarify this misunderstanding. The Berlin playwright was staying in a large hotel near the Tuileries, where I found him with his wife, his daughter and son, all blond, elegant, energetic, seeming to have transported into this palatial foyer the accelerated and impertinent rhythm of their Berlin milieu.

Sternheim admitted that he had simply forgotten the authorization he had given me a few months earlier. He had clearly come with the intention of conquering Paris, and to prepare his interviews with French publishers and theatre directors he had, he recounted to me, successfully bargained that very morning the apartment he occupied with his family and which they had begun by offering him at an exorbitant sum. The threatening letter he had sent André Berge was clearly part of the general plan of his offensive against the French capital and its theatres, an offensive whose objectives were never definitive and only partially achieved.

Sternheim was nervously shifting about, his conversation was choppy, biting like his prose. Robert de Traz said in his *Dépaysements*, which had just appeared,[7] that having asked a cultured Berliner to cite the best German writers of the hour, he received the following response: 'There are only two: Carl Sternheim and Thomas Mann. That's it.'

Carl Sternheim was probably not far from expressing the same opinion about himself and his contemporaries. His attitude suggested it. (Even if he may have had some reservations about Thomas Mann!) 'It's strange,' he confided to me, 'how lacking in certainties we are in France! So who are your real talents here? Giraudoux, Cocteau, Aragon, do you know? Is he any good?'

When I retorted that the same provisional uncertainty surely existed in Germany, he interjected commandingly: 'But not at all, you see! We are perfectly aware at home. It's true that you must ignore, here…'

I threw out a few names at random: 'Werfel, Döblin, Unruh…'

—'Who?'

—'Fritz von Unruh.'

—'Don't know him.'

—'The author of *Opfergang*.'[8]

—'This author is not known in Germany.'

—'And Rilke…'

—'There are perhaps young girls who still read him. But he is not, you understand, of our time…'.

With a decisive gesture, Sternheim adjusted his monocle, which froze his hard eye. His position was established. You had to accept it as it was, with the biases, the about-turns, the paradoxes and cutting cadence.

Half an hour later, when I returned home, I still had Sternheim's last wisecrack ringing in my ear when I found on the table a note which had just been delivered from the Hôtel Foyot.[9] It was Rilke, who had arrived in Paris the day before, alerting me to his arrival.

How happy I am to announce to you (finally!) I am close by in your neighbourhood. When will I see you? I was suffering rather these last months and I am still not in the best of shape. This is why, these first days in Paris, I shall be retiring early. Give me a sign and know that I am impatient to shake the hand that Malte has so wearied.

Sincerely yours, R.M. Rilke

At times I see once more the place where, the following day, I joined Rilke. For me it was only a matter of a few steps to reach the Hôtel Foyot. Beside the restaurant of the same name, in this quarter that only rarely comes alive with sessions of the Senate, or on Thursday evenings, the exit from the Jardin du Luxembourg, it was—and still is—a calm hotel with an almost provincial air. A gate gives access to an interior courtyard, covered with a glass roof, like those I have often encountered in Danish hotels.

That is where I waited for Rilke after being announced, and where I saw him approach me for the first time. He had these grey-blue eyes, this slightly pinched nose, the lofty brow that has often been remarked on, and that moustache drooping at the tapered tips, which at first glance suggested the Slavic or Oriental. He approached me with outstretched hand, with an eagerness dictated by his natural politeness, but a true joyfulness broke through as he led me to the left of the glass vestibule into a small salon to which French doors gave access. Behind us, some visiting English woman was occupied writing letters and we conversed in hushed tones. This presence of another made us uncomfortable, and almost right away Rilke suggested that I accompany him outside. I waited for him a few moments amongst the green plants and rattan armchairs in the foyer, then we walked down rue de Tournon together.

Rilke had this somewhat strange silhouette which I would become accustomed to seeing over the months that followed and which barely changed during his stay in Paris. He sported a grey felt hat, with round brim and flat base, light gaiters, suede gloves and a grey cloth overcoat: 'One of those martingale half-belted overcoats that you only see in Central Europe,' as Jean Cassou wrote, adding:

> He wore the uniform of the distant provinces from where he came to us... It was undoubtedly this disorientated ambiance that Malte Laurids Brigge paraded amongst us and which we must have seen with August Strindberg when he trundled his nightmares from hotel garni to hotel garni, from library to library and hospital to hospital.

For my part, I particularly recall the sense of astonishment I felt at the thought that my companion was really Rilke and that we were strolling together through this neighbourhood so familiar to Malte. So I only retained a scattering of memories of this first interview. That day, it was Rilke moreover who tended to question me. We had so much to catch up on, he said, that I could excuse his rather overbearing and indiscreet curiosity.

He seemed particularly interested in the fact that my Alsatian origin must have exercised a certain degree of stability throughout my youth, through being suspended between two languages, speaking one, writing my first lines of verse in another, drawn in turn by both poles. How could this bilingual formation have made of me a writer in the French language? What challenges had I faced? What place did they occupy in my spirit, the one then the other, these two languages? By posing such questions to me he was not so much thinking of himself, who had come to the French language by very different paths, but of the two young sons of his friend Baladine Klossowska, Balthus and Pierre,[10] who, raised first in Germany then Switzerland, were in a situation not dissimilar to mine and whose future concerned him.

Having descended to the *quais*, we returned by rue de Grenelle, stopping by the offices of the publisher Gallimard, where André Gide had deposited for safe keeping the box of books and papers that he had managed to save in 1914 and which contained all that remained of Rilke's last Parisian habitation on rue Campagne-Première.[11] Rilke arranged the time at which he would come to collect this parcel, then we walked on in the direction of the Luxembourg. I took leave of him on the rue Servandoni, before the porch of a house where friends were already waiting for him.

Unlike Sternheim, Rilke had not resolved to conquer Paris, but barely had he stepped off the train when Paris was already making appeals to him. Two different cities competed for his time and his spirit. There was the Paris of memories, the secret garden of his past to which he would like to return; and yet the salons were now demanding his presence, the telephone pursued him right into his room.

There was no longer any question of him living as in those former times, when he might take a quick lunch in the discreet shade of the terrace of Restaurant Jouven on boulevard Montparnasse, then immerse himself for hours on end in his world of phantoms and dreams, at that time when he sometimes postponed an appointment for several weeks, for fear that his thoughts might be unnecessarily disturbed, and when he confided to Clara Rilke that in the space of a month he had only spoken to two people: Rodin and Carrière.[12] They knew that he had experienced a peculiar contentment in undertaking a German translation of the poems of Paul Valéry and that he himself was the author of French poems which had just appeared in *Commerce*. They had read *The Notebooks of Malte Laurids Brigge* and had grasped the level of achievement.

This romantic poet, whose foreign work was locked away in an inaccessible domain, excited curiosity. Here was a unicorn gone astray in the botanical garden, which drew the gaze of women through its whiteness and mysterious eyes. And Rilke, whilst more or less resisting these overly diverse solicitations, was retained in Paris by a few tested friendships, by the taste—so contrary to other tendencies of his nature—which he always showed for a certain worldly cultivated atmosphere with the capacity to shelter him from his own profound temptations, and above all by the hope for that inner convalescence and moral renewal on which he had based this sojourn.

Rilke, in the first instance, had no intention of remaining in Paris for a matter of weeks. Despite the fatigue that the stay in Paris caused him, despite the physical and moral disappointment that came over him all too soon and was to leave him with the impression of a 'drawn-out defeat', he ended up staying on there from the beginning of January to the middle of August. 'Valéry is filled with friendship towards me,' something he never forgot to mention in his first letters as being prime amongst the reasons which detained him; but after long months of solitude he had soon begun feeling like 'an incorrigible country dweller' amidst the Parisian tumult.

I saw him at first only intermittently, then ever more frequently. Our interviews became a daily occurrence when Rilke proposed rereading with me the translation of the *Notebooks* before it was delivered to the printer. It was as a result of those months working together and these conversations that I have guarded the most vital and precise image of him.

VII

THE LUXEMBOURG, THE HÔTEL BIRON, MUZOT

Before taking his leave, Rilke had promised a visit to my home. He came on the agreed day, early in the afternoon. It was one of those white days at the end of winter sometimes granted Parisians, and Rilke's first words were to express wonder at the view he encountered from our fifth floor.[1]

Before our eyes was spread the Jardin du Luxembourg, lost to sight in its wintry bareness beneath the interlacing black web of the branches. To the left, in the tangle of dead trees, the triple basins of the *fontaine Médicis*, with reflections playing on its pool. But at the garden's centre the larger basin shimmered, having absorbed the entire sky, a smear of light that travelled around from a distance the grey ribbon of the balustrade. Rilke loved this situation, which placed us, he said, '*on the same level as the sky*'.

He also liked that the apartment was separated from the street below by the balcony which ran along the entire façade, so that we could imagine ourselves raised aloft above the city, to a great height, as in a balloon basket, and that even leaving the windows open we enjoyed a feeling of isolation and intimacy.

He spoke to us of his Parisian domiciles, which had changed so often, and which he recalled with impressions of dread, tenderness or melancholy.

There was rue Toullier,[2] where he had felt the human density of the great city in a way that was overly oppressive, where a dozen windows from a neighbouring house had turned their dark gaze on him, at once mysterious and indiscreet.

There was rue Cassette,[3] where he really did have a student neighbour, as recounted in the *Notebooks*, whose nervous condition prevented him from preparing for his exams.

There was the house in Meudon,[4] where he had lived in wretched discomfort, at the mercy of all the inclement weather, but in silent proximity to Rodin's immense objects.

Finally, there was the high rotunda of the Hôtel Biron,[5] with its magnificent wood panelling, where he had succeeded Clara Rilke.

In rue Cassette, he had always enjoyed the scattering of trees in the little enclosed garden of the parish of Saint-Sulpice, whose calm at certain times was reminiscent of a beguinage. Before residing on rue de l'Abbé de l'Épée,[6] he had almost let himself be tempted by a hotel on the corner of boulevard Saint-Michel and rue Denfert-Rochereau, whose windows also overlooked the Luxembourg. But his most beautiful sojourns had been at the Hôtel Biron, which he had occupied at successive times—due to his frequent travels and absences—in several different wings and floors, and to which he was the first to draw Rodin's attention.

The park of the Hôtel Biron was not then the classic French garden, with its paths and side paths, its water jets and quincunxes, that the curator of the Musée Rodin, Georges Grappe, virtually reconstructed according to the plans of Blondel.[7] Abandoned for close on a century to the caprices of unhinged vegetation, the beautiful garden of the Duchesse du Maine[8] had been transformed into a magnificent jungle of brambles, wild grasses, viburnums, poppies, ivy and wild rose bushes, which overflowed on to the terrace.

In this *Paradou*[9] Rilke had as neighbours Jean Cocteau, the actor de Max and the Count of Osnowicine, who organized sometimes noisy nocturnal parties. One day de Max, who took great pleasure in sumptuous fantasies, had the idea of installing a bathroom in the sacristy of the disused chapel belonging to the Hôtel. This lit the touchpaper for a scandal which ultimately forced the administration to dismiss the most recently installed tenants of the Hôtel Biron. Only Rodin, who occupied the central pavilion, endured and following a prolonged struggle managed to secure the freedom of the Hôtel, in exchange for the legacy he left to the state of his entire sculptural oeuvre.

Rilke did not only relish recalling the circumstances of his stay at the Hôtel Biron; he also knew intimately the history of the beautiful palace he had revealed to Rodin. There the Duchesse du Maine had held spectacular parties, Tsar Paul I had come with his wife to admire the porticos, the groves and flower gardens of *le maréchal* Biron, André Chénier had perhaps met there his beloved 'young captive' de Coigny...[10] Russia, the French eighteenth century, poetry meets Rodin, the great admiration of Rilke, beneath the shade of these old lime trees, in this wild park, swarming with rabbits and birds.

Whatever corner of Paris he was opining on, it seemed that Rilke's words summoned to life this backdrop of characters and memories, which for him remained unsullied, outside of time, whether it was the Louvre or Notre-Dame, the faubourg Saint-Germain or Sainte-Chapelle. He said to my wife that day,

I am most fearful that you may not be quite sensitive enough to the astonishing privilege of living before this beautiful Palais du Luxembourg and to have Marie de Médicis for a neighbour.

We returned to the room, lit by a wood fire, and Rilke, at the sight of this blaze, revealed that pleasure which he customarily showed before all those elements which lend to life an intimate or traditional countenance.

At Muzot he had only a large earthenware stove, he said. Sometimes he missed Switzerland and this living presence of a fire that the hearth alone could grant us.

We asked him about the Valais, about his ancient tower, his life at Muzot. He told us how this old manor house with its thick walls, like a hard shell, had made him fearful at first, to the point that he could not imagine that it might be possible for him to settle there in any stable fashion. But thanks to the taste and ingenuity of Baladine Klossowska, who had, during the early months of the summer, been present through this somewhat rigorous first stay, the old tower had become more hospitable, with its rose bushes, apple trees and its high poplar, positioned at the fore, like a lookout watching the open sea.[11]

He spoke of those harsh and lonely winters through the course of which he had, thanks to unprecedented concentration, found the inspiration to resume the *Elegies*, then of the Valais spring, which came with an almost Italian suddenness, literally sucking up from the ground the frail anemones, soon to fade;[12] how he resumed his relations with the inhabitants of the country. They were simple folk, but so naturally inclined towards mysterious things that the very word *superstition* did not have the same sense for them. It was this trait of their character above all which had attracted him and which allowed a natural familiarity with them.

He told us that the peasants he met on his walks sometimes questioned him about the ghosts which, according to tradition, reputedly haunted old Muzot. They asked him for news of Jean de Montheys, who had once lived in the manor house and who had fallen at Marignan, as well as his wife Isabelle. One or the other must, according to popular legend, appear on occasion at Muzot.

'Has it been a long time since you've seen her again, the lady of the château? How is she doing?' an old peasant woman enquired of him. Rilke was not surprised by such questions, for had he not, more than once, heard the door close behind Isabelle de Chevron and had he not brushed against her one evening, in the dark hallway?

He told us of the chatelaine of Muzot: after the death of her husband, two suitors, of equal nobility and virile beauty, vied for her hand. As she could not decide on one over the other, they fought a duel and both died from the wounds inflicted during their terrible combat. Isabelle lost her reason and her tormented soul has been roaming the cemetery of Miège and the old manor ever since.

Rilke told us many other stories. They were examples of the astonishing prescience of time possessed by the peasants of Miège. Another legend was that of the Château de Bellevue, now a hotel, favoured by Rilke to house his guests, an ancient house in the centre of Sierre which also had its fair share of strange happenings and apparitions. Then there was a curious sound, like the path a worm makes through wood, that Rilke sometimes heard in his study and which he described with such an insistence and precision that we thought quite definitely we could hear it, and we all kept quiet to listen to the very faint sighing of a damp log in the fireplace.

Emmanuel Bove[13] had passed by to see me during the afternoon and joined us. The three of us listened to Rilke, recollecting without end, drawing around us a fine-spun net of memories and phantoms in which he himself seemed imprisoned.

———

Then came the beautiful season *valaisanne*,[14] so special because of the dry climate of this country, the high winds which swept away all the clouds, with an almost too-violent sun which made the buds burst like champagne corks. This sun was the signal for the visits which, staggered from Sunday to Sunday, put an end to Rilke's protracted confinement. He had the impression of exiting a winter burrow, and around him unfurled with its hills, its castles and churches, responding to one another far and wide, the clear and airy landscape of that *valaisanne* valley whose mountains had never oppressed him.[15]

One of the visitors whom Rilke most joyfully welcomed was Paul Valéry, who, travelling to Italy via the Simplon Pass, had stopped off in Sierre to meet his German translator. Rilke spoke to us of his gratitude towards the French poet. He had come to his poetic oeuvre relatively late, but, precisely because he had suddenly discovered the beauties of Valéry's work, he was indebted to him for the decisive shock which had both stimulated and prepared him for that fruitful winter when he was able to complete the *Duino Elegies* and write the *Sonnets to Orpheus*.

Rilke was very struck at that moment to learn that Valéry had recommenced writing after a silence of twenty-five years. He who suffered since 1914 from an incapacity to express himself had felt intimately reassured in discovering the dense beauty and 'so wonderfully rested' poetry of Valéry.

THE LUXEMBOURG, THE HÔTEL BIRON, MUZOT

Paul Valéry had visited Rilke in April 1924, and despite all that could have separated them they felt a strong attraction to each other. A few years later Valéry was to express the surprise he had felt before the 'enchanted tower of Muzot', whose 'frightening peace' and 'grandeur of tranquillity' had at first gripped his heart. For Rilke, this meeting had been a joyful relaxation. The freest trust was quick to inspire the words of the two poets. The charm of Valéry's conversation, his wit, his lively cheerfulness quickly dissipated whatever remained of the shadows and ghosts in the lower rooms of Muzot. Rilke spoke of those contented hours with that finely nuanced humour in which he excelled in conversation, and he lent an almost comical colour to the companionship of that day.

Rilke's manner of storytelling was such that, without it being possible to doubt the accuracy of his words, we were not however required to admit their literal meaning.

I noticed that certain stories he recounted on separate occasions to different people were not always expressed in the same terms. I don't believe that these differences are solely down to the person, the witness who quoted Rilke's words, not the infidelity of his memory. It seemed to me rather that the stories he told, which were oft repeated, ended up assuming an ever more dramatic depth, a clarity which better elucidated the meaning of the anecdote.

Sometimes the listener also had some influence on the tone of the unfolding story. Rilke, who wielded such power over his listeners in private, was also subject to their influence. An exchange took place between himself and his interlocuters and he needed to feel the presence and attention of others to be properly assured.

It has been said that his politeness, so refined and delicate, was a defence against others. On the other hand, when he felt truly at ease he revealed in his conversation a charming spontaneity and sense of abandon.

This is the impression Rilke gave us that day, by recounting with an almost exuberant cheerfulness the adventures of this visit by Valéry. At the time of the French poet's departure the two friends were joking, having fun like schoolboys on holiday. Rilke claimed that the railway porter had wanted to send Valéry's suitcase at '*petite vitesse*' because he had seen on it the initials P.V. This comical mistake gave rise to joking on both sides and must have in any case relieved any sense of sadness at this moment of departure…

But we suddenly realized that hours had passed whilst Rilke held us under the spell of his tales. Darkness had long since fallen and we hadn't even noticed the drum announcing the closure of the Luxembourg. It was eight o'clock. Rilke rose to his feet and we moved no less abruptly in terms of conventional politeness. He left, leaving behind him this strange universe, populated by peasants, ghosts and peals of laughter, which he had evoked and which would surely not fade as swiftly as the embers of the dying fire in the hearth.

VIII

MORNINGS WORKING ON *THE NOTEBOOKS OF MALTE*

During one of our following interviews, which must have been confused in my memory with this first visit, we talked about my translation of the *Notebooks*, which I had just completed. I suggested that Rilke cast an eye over it. It was then that he asked me if I would agree to devote some mornings to reading my manuscript to him myself, which would perhaps be the best way to collaborate on its development and to enjoy our close neighbourliness without undue haste or fatigue. This offer was too tempting for me not to readily accept.

In Muzot, Rilke was of the habit, he informed me, of devoting mornings to his correspondence, to reading or to short walks. It was only in the afternoon that he addressed his most important works:

The morning is a closed space, limited by waking and a meal. Its freshness can leave favourable impressions, but it is hardly conducive to an enterprise of any scope. In contrast, the afternoon allows me to follow as far as possible an idea or an inspiration. I can have the evening, if necessary the whole night, if by chance the momentum continues. The morning is cut off by the meal which invariably limits it. But the afternoon—above all in my Muzot solitude—led into the infinitude of night and thus was the true domain of fruitful dreams.

By choosing the morning hours for our daily encounters, Rilke indicated that he considered them as relaxation rather than a task: passing into a peaceful realm of conversation and friendship. It was also, in the busy schedule of his Parisian days, an opportunity to escape the past, an alibi, an hour of perspective and respite, devoted to a book which remained the most cherished of all to him.

———

Rilke arrived at my apartment, usually a little after ten o'clock, sometimes later. When the bell rang at eleven o'clock, it generally meant that he was taking advantage of the fine weather and had crossed the Luxembourg, whose open gate, almost opposite his hotel, renewed every morning the same temptation. From this short walk, he would bring back some wholly fresh impression from the inexhaustible charm of this garden, or some sardonic and penetrating observation about a face he had encountered.

He never missed one of our meetings without alerting me through a brief note, delivered in the morning or the evening of the day before to inform me that some impediment or feeling of malaise had obliged him to postpone our '*reading hour, which I can assure you will be sorely missed*', he had the politeness to add. There were sometimes too many commitments in his Parisian life, so much so that he complained of not being able to effectively '*organize and control*' his time.

Towards the end of April, it was a flu that kept him bedridden for a week or so, but the resulting fatigue following the days of fever dragged on into the middle of May.

With a few interruptions, our collaboration continued in this way for several months. I am confident I did nothing to shorten it. But I am not far from suspecting Rilke too of a secret indulgence to prolong these conversations to which he brought, as the weeks passed by, more freedom and withdrawal from his social obligations.

This daily visit customarily took place as follows. I received Rilke in a large room from which two French doors open on to the balcony of our fifth floor. We would take our places facing each other, on either side of a small card table covered with green cloth. From where we were sat, by the window, we could see the treetops of the Luxembourg and, by leaning just a little, the bright spot of the basin at the centre of the garden.

Rilke drew from the small brown leather briefcase which always accompanied it a copy of the German edition of the *Notebooks*, bound in grey. I opened the manuscript of my translation at the page where we had left off the previous day. I read the French text aloud. Rilke followed from the German text. From time to time he interrupted me to make some remark, to give an explanation or to ask me to reread a passage.

———

The surest reminder I have retained of these meetings are not so much the quick notes that I took in the moment as the text of the *Notebooks*, in whose margin Rilke's words were inscribed for me. Some of them blended in so well with the text that we read together that I can't be sure if a detail appears in the *Notebooks* or if it issued from myself. Sometimes I have to leaf through the book to convince myself that I am not the sole custodian of this story or that scene which he had already written before lending them his voice, and through his manipulation an even more expressive life.

When I reopen the *Notebooks*, what first rises from these pages is the peculiar atmosphere of Paris: the rue de Seine and rue de l'Ancienne-Comédie, with their houses in states of demolishment, rue Saint-Jacques with its greengrocers, its creameries, its charcoal merchants and sordid bistros, to that greener and more aerated quarter of the hospitals and delivery wards around Val-de-Grâce and the Hôpital Cochin.

It was in these two directions that his steps had led the young Rilke when he settled into his room in rue Toullier, and these first impressions dominate the whole book. But he began by enduring this Paris like a malaise, suffering its most painful aspects, its most cruelly human hours: '*It was a city thick as a brush*,' Rilke said.

> *Malte was naturally unaware of all this. Otherwise, how could he have dared to expose himself to such experiences, how would he have placed himself before them? But all this was perhaps already in some way contained within him: his childhood, that encounter with the man, one evening in the street, his fears, his terrors...*
>
> *This is undoubtedly why he had to discover before the others these strangely faded beings, these wrecks borne away by the irresistible flow of the great city. That is why they attract him like the very faces of his temptation. The mysterious sign of this woman who seems to call him, this prayer that he murmurs which has no other meaning...*

I slowly reread these first pages to Rilke—without omitting those at the beginning which he already knew—and he listens to me, leant over his book, concentrated in his effort to reclaim his old vision. '*I went out, I saw*'. '*Saw*', repeats Rilke, accentuating as if in spite of himself this repetition which underlines Malte's first discoveries. '*These things*', he explains,

> *enter into him through all the senses: sight first, then hearing, and only then he learns how to use them. He learns how to see, he also learns how to hear: what is there and above all what is not there: the absence of noise, the absence of sight, the absence of face… Now, it is sometimes precisely this non-visible element, this absence which offers him the key to things.*

I notice that the words 'live', 'noises', 'see' and 'fear' each appear at the top of the first paragraphs, like keys indicating the tone of these first pieces. Rilke approves:

> *To live, to see, fear, these are the themes of the first variations on the Malte experience. And each summons its opposite, which reveals its true meaning: 'So this is where people come to live? I would rather be more inclined to believe that this is where they come to die.' 'Certainly, there are noises. But there is something here that is far more terrible: the silence.' 'I am learning to see. But I don't know why everything is penetrating me more deeply.' Opposition—and at the same time secret relationship—between appearance and profound reality, between everyday life and the inexpressible. Contrast which is summed up in the final sentence, verging on the ironic, where it is a question of the hansom cabs that bear the dying to hospital: hired by the hour at the usual rate: two francs per hour of agony.*

Following this path, we hesitated a moment over the translation of the word *Bekanntschaften*. As I ran through at random 'Acquaintances, relations, friends…' Rilke interjected almost vehemently: '*Let's leave friends out of the running right away. Friends, Malte had none!*'

If I rightly interpret the mark made on my manuscript, we had chosen not to push on much further with our reading. After discussing his initial impressions of Paris, Rilke had come to talk to me about this other double of his hero, Sigbjørn Obstfelder.[1] The book lying open on the table, Rilke explained.

Sigbjørn Obstfelder was a Norwegian writer whom he had discovered by chance through his wide reading. He was a poet of subtle impressionism, possessed of an acute sensitivity. His *Diary of a Priest* is the story of a soul who, in his desperate attempts to come closer to God, on the contrary moves further and further away, prey to a cerebral fever which leaves him increasingly exasperated. However, Rilke only knew Obstfelder through a handful of poems, before two circumstances in the poet's life struck him: the first was that Obstfelder had lived in Paris, the second that he had died at age thirty-two, and thus no doubt not having the opportunity to inform his work with the full reach of his tormented and generous soul. These are the two circumstances above all which gradually imposed the form of the young Obstfelder on to the spirit of Rilke, from the moment when he felt the need to express his strange experience of Paris and considered incarnating him as an imaginary hero.

Rilke was already enjoying Jacobsen in lieu of discovering Kierkegaard and he had even learnt Danish to better gain access to these works. Nevertheless, despite all that attracted him to the French capital, Jacobsen still felt a stranger there and, contrastingly, he became more conscious of his Nordic origins. Also, when his Parisian notes began to take form, it became obvious to him that his hero must be a compatriot of Jacobsen and recollections of Danish readings suggested the name of Malte.

However, Rilke did not immediately design the *Notebooks* in the form we now know.

The figure of Malte was pursuing me, [he told me] *but I realized that I only had an incomplete knowledge of him, and in some respects one entirely external. That is why, when I began to write this book which at first appeared to me as a sort of counterpart to the* Stories of God,[2] *I used the dialogue form, which I employed to evoke Ewald and his friend. I was far from suspecting at that time what development this work would undergo and what imprint my Parisian experience would ultimately impose on it.*

I was then in Rome. I had been living for some months in a small artist's studio that was made available to me in Strohl-Fern Park.[3] The reading of Jacobsen at the same time as this Italian spring, disappointing by its excess of haste, had given me a nostalgia for those countries of the North where I still only knew the good Ellen Key, to whom I dedicated the Stories of God.[4] *I wrote a series of dialogues between a young man and a young girl, who confided their little secrets to each other. It happened that the young man spoke at some length to the young daughter of a Danish poet he had known, a certain Malte, who died very young, in Paris. The young girl wanted to know more and the young man had the imprudence to tell her that his friend had left a diary which he pretended never to have been aware of. The young girl insisted that he show it to her.*

For a few days, [Rilke continued] *I managed to convince her to be patient under various pretexts. But the young girl's curiosity knew no bounds and she began to imagine Malte in her own way. I realized that I could not equivocate any longer. Interrupting my dialogue, I began to write the journal of Malte himself, without further concerning myself with the secondary characters, who, almost in spite of myself, delivered him up to me.*

However, Rilke realized that to draw the invisible figure of Malte it would still require infinite images, memories, sensitive reflections of this imaginary life. Malte's childhood he seemed to know, but shouldn't he have verified it in some way on location, in this Danish land where castles, ponds, parks, trees, everywhere so close and significant, composed a strangely alluring atmosphere? Rilke had in mind Copenhagen, the castles on the verdant island of Funen, Thisted, where Jacobsen lived; and he finally convinced himself that he really had to get to know Denmark first-hand when an invitation suddenly arrived from Sweden, concerning Ellen Key's series of conferences on his work, handing him the opportunity to make such a journey. Without waiting another day he set off by train.

Dictated by such a profound need, which had only expressed itself through singular detours, the *Notebooks* were, however, still far from finding their definitive form. Rilke explained to me:

I have always written very rapidly, whilst in some sense undergoing the improvisation of a rhythm which sought its vital form through me. When this movement is within us, expression is no longer just a matter of obedience. That was how I wrote the Cornet[5] *in a single night, reproducing in an irresistible way the images that the reflections of the setting sun had projected on the clouds that I saw passing by my open window.*

Many of my New Poems[6] *are somehow written by themselves, sometimes several in one day, in the definitive form, and when I wrote* The Book of Hours[7] *I had the impression that so easy had the trigger been that I could no longer stop myself writing. Moreover,* The Book of Hours *is not a collection from which we would detach a page or a poem like picking a flower. More than any of my other books it is a song, a unique poem, where each stanza is in its place, impossible to modify, like the veins on a leaf, like the voices of a choir.*

I remember [Rilke told me again] *that after* The Book of Hours *I imagined I could only write poems having such a powerful unity. (And it is true that I have tried to give the same unity to the* Duino Elegies *and to the* Sonnets to Orpheus: *no doubt it is in part this need for unity which has so delayed the completion of the* Elegies.*)*

But when I began to write The Notebooks of Malte Laurids Brigge, *things were initially quite different. The necessary unity was no longer that of the poem, it was that of this character who had to be made to live, from one end to the other, in life's infinite diversity. It was a chopped-up, fractured rhythm that imposed itself on me, and I was led in a number of unforeseen directions. Sometimes they were childhood memories, sometimes Paris, sometimes the Danish atmosphere, sometimes images which appeared to have no connection with my character himself. I almost confused myself with Malte, I had lost sight of him, a journey away seemed to draw him out of reach, but on returning to Paris I suddenly found him more present than ever.*

I had written many pages at random. Some were letters, others notes, journal fragments, prose poems. Despite the tight web of this for me completely new prose, it was a development through trial and error, of groping forward in a blind procession that never seemed to come to an end. But ultimately it turned out that he was still there, this companion of so many nights, this friend and confidant.

He had accompanied me to Venice, he had roamed like me through the streets of Paris, he had lingered in the Alyscamps and crossed paths with the shepherds of Les Baux.[8] *I had seen him in Copenhagen, on the Langelinie, we had met in the avenues of yews in Fredensborg, he remembered the sweet scent of phlox in summer, his childhood was mine, he was me, and yet he was someone else.*

Of so many evils that we had both lived through, I had gradually and painfully burdened him. That had kept me at a distance from him, and for a while I would end up by forgetting it all. But remained conjoined by a common secret, by the sensitive parts of a wound which has not yet healed.

IX

THE LOST PAGES OF
THE NOTEBOOKS OF MALTE

Depending on the day, we laboured with more or less application and Rilke showed himself more or less willing to confidences. The sole control of the translation, which led him to define certain words, to specify their relationships or their value in a sentence, obliged him to issue me with a good number of clarifications. For example, an adverb or brief incident omitted and whose importance he underlined. Perhaps it was a question of painting Beethoven that the poet imagines in the Thebaid[1] before his solitary instrument, amongst the mountains of the desert and where I had written 'The Bedouins would flee on their horses superstitiously', Rilke was quick to point out an oversight: '*One must not forget "far off" because no one is visible around him who plays.*'

And this detail, far from forming a pleonasm, in fact reinforced the evocation of this storm of music around which only a few lions prowl at a distance, excited by their blood. Then I had translated '*sich niederschlägt*' as 'settles', which Rilke rightly advised me to change to 'condenses', a term closer to chemistry and thus a more precisely nuanced translation. And when in this same section

I hesitated over the most suitable translation of '*Feuerschein*', he simply observed: '*Imagine a laboratory that would only be lit by the fires of a stove. How would we say that?*'

Whilst striving to keep the text as close as possible to the original, Rilke never ignored the difficulties inherent in the language itself and the dissimilarities of vocabularies:

As you have sensed, the 'nuances' are insufficient. Die Übergänge*: transitions, the passage of one nuance to another. But all this is extremely difficult to render. I know you have to settle for something.*

The rigorous precision of a version could, in certain cases, depend on the place assigned to a word in the sentence. In the presence of a page where Malte's mother describes the face of Ingeborg, Rilke sets out by explaining:

This passage means that in describing a woman, we do not only have the one means of rendering it visible: to paint all that surrounds it, to leave it blank, in the middle.

He then applies himself to improving my version. I wrote, by following the text, that which precisely locates the limit at which all attempts to describe the face of a woman meet: 'until a certain place where everything stopped, slowly and one might say cautiously, to the envelopment of a light contour...'. Rilke suggests:

It might be better to let this precise contour form by what it encloses it, and only to say this at the close of the sentence it envelops.

And thus we arrived at the following translation: 'To a certain place where everything stopped, stopped gently and so to speak, cautiously, to the light contour which enveloped it and which was never redrawn.'

These remarks—which in appearance were mere detail—renewed the lesson that certain of Rilke's letters had taught me, with that persuasive force and subtle authority which emanated from the poet's very presence. The man who spoke in this way was the writer who, in spite of his faith in the power of interior dictation, knew the secrets and resources of language and who could not bear to see the 'beautiful craft' exercised in a negligent or wanting manner. But sometimes his explanations caused me to penetrate still further, even into that mysterious zone where the work develops and which the writer is the only one to have knowledge of.

Speaking once more of Ingeborg, Rilke remarked for example on a sentence where it was the question of the strange perfection in the smile of the dying girl:

We should almost wish for a closer equivalence here to restore the complete independence of this smile which has no external goal.

Then, concerning the exclamation by which the young girl betrays her weariness of life:

It's not so much the sound of her voice that she wants to hear, but the tone of it, the sonority of her astonishing confession: by hearing it, she realizes, you might say, the state of her soul concealed from everyone and in small measure from herself.

This passage had previously been translated by André Gide, and I hesitated for a long time before taking up the version that the author of *Nourritures terrestres* had given in *La Nouvelle Revue française* of this exclamation: '*Ich mag nicht mehr*' (I don't like it any more) to '*J'ai mon content*' (I have had my fill of it).

From his very first reading of my text, Rilke baulked at this translation:

> *Dare I say* [he wrote to me] *that I am not happy at all with this*: '*I have had my fill of it*'. *Wouldn't Ingeborg rather have said, 'I cannot bear any more'? I suggest you reflect on it; for me—and it's difficult for me to judge—this 'I have had my fill of it' feels somehow jarring, it seems stilted compared to the perfect simplicity of this unexpected confession. But you must make your own judgements without giving too much importance to my remark…*

In formulating these reservations, Rilke was unaware that I could shelter behind the authority of Gide. He let me be the judge, and I ultimately retained Gide's version. However, I believe it was Rilke who was right.

Sometimes his comments gave a glimmering of memory, some notable occasion in his life. As with those old worn-out men whom he compared to figureheads, wizened, faded by the sun and rain, who draw the birds to them and throw them crumbs in the Paris gardens:

> *These are the figureheads, once part of a ship and which we have become accustomed to planting in the earth, the only piece that survives from the boat, like ornamentation in those poor gardens of the North coast.*

And more moving still was this memory, through which Rilke, momentarily confusing his own mother with that of Malte, clarified his vision:

No, Mother doesn't hide her face, she raises her hands to her temples and closes her eyes, her face is closed shut by the closed eyes, but at the same time quite transparent; she closes her eyes to no longer see what she had seen, but the vision of the event she is going to recount arises in her and kindles in her this memory, which, already, radiates from her through her closed face...

When talking to me about the genesis of the *Notebooks*, Rilke told me one day that he had not assembled all the fragments and notes originally intended for this work. This was deliberate, for he wished to lend it the impression of an unfinished work, the testament of a young man who, like this Sigbjørn Obstfelder who occupied his thoughts, would not have time to come fully to fruition. But some fragments were missing for other reasons: there were certain manuscripts that Rilke had, with carefree largesse, bestowed on friends and which had subsequently been lost.

One day he regaled me with the account of such an episode when a manuscript had been lost, temporarily or permanently. It was one of those spring mornings of whose images we encounter a good number through the course of the *Notebooks*. Malte had descended boulevard Saint-Michel and was following the *quai* in the direction of Notre-Dame. This *cour des Miracles*,[2] which has since vanished, attracted him like so many other mysterious corners of Paris where he had encountered, in its surroundings and along its winding lanes leading to the church of Saint-Julien-le-Pauvre, more than one of those disinherited beings who traverse the *Notebooks* and the *New Poems*.

But on that particular day, as he followed the *quai*, Rilke, or Malte, suddenly noticed in front of him a couple of very young lovers who walked without seeing anything other than the reflection of each other in their eyes. They moved slowly, so slow in fact that Malte, in spite of himself, so as to not disturb them, in turn slowed his own pace.

Malte had begun following them and he could observe them all the more quietly as, for them, he did not seem to even exist. The image of this happiness drew him in its wake and he couldn't detach his gaze, taking nourishment in silence, as if the youth and naivety of the couple had communicated with him. '*So this is how we love*,' he said to himself, and memories rose up in him from the far distance, memories that were perhaps regrets.

The couple continued their walk. Malte passed into the shadows of the plane trees, which did not yet cast a network of infinitely delicate shadows upon the pavement—more reflections than a drawing—at times almost invisible. Somewhere a window opened, but the couple were brighter than all the windows in all the streets of Paris. The two lovers passed on to a bridge, Malte still following them, and suddenly, looking up, he saw an inscription on an entrance gate: *La Morgue*. (It was the old morgue at the eastern extremity of Île de la Cité which has since been replaced by a square.)

Malte could now have continued on his way, but, no less than the two lovers, he did not hesitate. The couple entered the large, cool chamber where the public were admitted to recognize the drowned and the unidentified dead, destined for autopsy. Here were the curious, a silent woman, tourists who had entered by chance; you might have thought it a church or museum but for the barely suspicious odour, vaguely sweetish suggesting the vault or a naturalist's collection. It seemed to Malte that he had experienced that same odour when passing, near to his home, that shop on the rue de l'École-de-Médecine, where a man was busy reconstituting a skeleton, dipping every so often into a pile of collarbones, jaws and vertebrae.

However, the two lovers did not even seem to notice this odour, nor suspect how their presence in this place might seem surprising. From time to time they paused and, faces still lit by the smile that they had just exchanged, considered these large inert dolls with a look of distraction or vague surprise. They had just stopped for the third time when Malte saw the young man's hand, with a barely perceptible movement, squeeze the bare arm of the young girl, who started. She took a step aside, so their faces found themselves regarding one another, and all of a sudden they kissed.

Despite the spontaneity of the gesture, it seemed to Malte that there was something clumsy about this kiss, artificial, almost forced, as if they had been in some way constrained. The contrast seemed too calculatedly uncouth to him, and he told himself that a careful artist would probably have avoided such coincidence. His gaze, however, remained suspended on the nape of the young girl's neck, where a light blonde lock quivered. Then his eyes returned to the corpse that lay before the young people. Half-absent, he considered these over-large feet, to which the dress lent inadequate covering, these swollen hands, this swollen face. Hair, mechanically his gaze searched the hair.

Suddenly he was afraid and understood: this pale and swollen dead woman was a young girl like the other. The swelling of death had not sufficiently altered her features that he would not be tempted to recognize her and to turn round in order to compare...

Naturally, I only succeed imperfectly in reproducing the story that Rilke recounted to me then with that acerbic precision which divined the very presence of the terrible. I no longer remember what Malte did next. Perhaps he went to seek refuge in the Bibliothèque

Sainte-Geneviève, where *Les Chroniques de Froissart*[3] introduced him to another world, perhaps he first tried to calm himself by following in the little square of Notre-Dame the infinitely criss-crossed design left in the sand by pigeons' feet.

Perhaps the fragment stopped there and Rilke was unable to speak of it further. It is more than likely that there are other episodes concerning Malte that we will happen on again one day. There were some which were written after the publication of the *Notebooks*, for though he had liberated himself almost violently, Rilke continued to live in a certain intimacy with his hero. Mme Albert-Lasard[4] told me that in 1914 in Munich she had received from him a book of prose which resembled Malte in tone, but which, unfortunately, after the war she left behind in a Zurich hotel room and it was never found. Lou Andreas-Salomé, who received letters from Rilke, certain passages of which found their way with slight variations into the *Notebooks*, cites in her memoirs the fragment of a diary Rilke sent her from Ronda in 1913 and which reveals that the universe of Malte had not vanished entirely for Rilke and continued to put forth this curious flowering.

In these lost or unknown pages, it could be that the Luxembourg occupies a central place. As I remarked one day to Rilke, this garden, which was so dear to him, is never—save the passage of the birds—described directly in the *Notebooks*. The walks of Malte only lead him past its gates, on the outside, as if Rilke wished to avoid involving this garden, which he paints with such tenderness and freshness in his letters, in the painful experiences of his hero. Nowhere described, it is merely evoked by allusion, it is '*infinitely tu*', as the '*plus cher désir*' of the lady of the tapestries of the unicorn in the Musée de Cluny.

Nevertheless, the atmosphere of this Jardin du Luxembourg Rilke loved to summon, and it occupied an important place in our conversations. With what delicate humour he spoke to me of one of his encounters: the little pensioner, for example, who read *Les Annales*[5] whilst strolling along the esplanade, or the old woman who was sat on a bench, eating a brioche, her hands diving into her drawstring bag; and how many others.

The author Léon Daudet somewhere makes the distinction between the Luxembourg of students and the Luxembourg as a place for sentimental outpourings, then the Luxembourg of families, where he and his friends experienced a feeling of 'gentrification'. This distinction would doubtless have borne little reality in the eyes of Rilke. For him the Luxembourg was an entity, a living and indivisible world, with its benches, its flowers, its humanity ever renewed. Yet he admitted to a predilection for certain more intimate spots, such as the rose enclosure near the museum and those corners along the balustrades from which one could overlook the centre of the garden, leant against the oleanders, in the reposeful and somewhat haughty vicinity of Marguerite de Provence, Anne of Austria or Valentine de Milan.

These reserves of solitude, at the heart of the crowd, and in an eternally civilized setting which at the same time remained open to the sky—this was what enchanted Rilke about the Luxembourg. One day he told me of an encounter he had there whose recollection still enthralled him. It was a little old woman, sitting on a bench in one of the more animated corners of the garden. Beside her, behind her, in front of her, everywhere there were people. Children were playing with hoops, groups of students were calling out to each other and laughing, women chattered away. But the little old woman had placed before her a box filled with photographs, trinkets and mementos.

Children darted past, balls bounced on the sand, the wind caused the sails to flap on the little yachts on the pond. But she had eyes only for her little box from which, one by one, she lifted images of First Communion, coloured postcards, keys, jewellery boxes, old photographs, scraps of ribbon that she gazed at and handled tenderly.

'*She was there,*' said Rilke, '*as if alone in the world, with her memories and thoughts*'.

When he made his way back she was still there, apparently still occupied in her absorbing work. The following day Rilke returned to this same bench, in the hope of seeing her once more. But instead of the little old woman he found only a nanny, portly and placid, who was cradling a child. Rilke moved on without delay, since he imagined that this woman, rotund as a tower, with her dress of voluminous folds, must have crushed beneath her weight all the fragile objects he had seen the day before, so lovingly arranged on this bench.

X

IN THE ENVIRONS OF THE PRINCESS

RILKE SOMETIMES ARRIVED LATE, complaining that people pursued him right into his hotel. Grand ladies and beautiful friends who sought his presence at their receptions called him by telephone first thing in the morning. Since Rilke would not have this device in his room, he was obliged to rush down a cold corridor to the nearest public phone. So commenced a comedy which he recounted and mimed with comic despair.

At the other end of the line, some exquisite woman, ensconced in her warm boudoir—or perhaps in her bedroom, the device sat on her bed—talked, talked on endlessly, in a languorous pose. At this pleasant hour, in the half-light of a snug room, there are a thousand things that beg to be spoken of, which demand to be entrusted without a moment's delay via this wonderfully docile medium of expression that is the telephone. If these words were not spoken right away, what intimate dramas would be forfeit? The malignant nature of these things, however, dictates that they do not from the outset present themselves clearly ordered, easy to summarize. Instead they gush out in jets, one after the other, wave upon wave. Ten times we are on the point of hanging up, and ten times an idea suddenly emerges at this precise instant, seductive and requiring new words: exclamations, slanderous asides, kind attentiveness, promises, compliments or gentle reproaches...

However, on the end of the line is a poor man, hauled in spite of himself from his room into a corridor crossed by draughts of cold air. A door slammed, a broom fell over, a cloud of dust rose up. Rilke coughed, feeling chilled: '*Certainly, dear princess, but...*' In vain he was trying to close the floodgates of an overly generous friendship. Neck resting softly on silk cushions, lower arm exposed by the low cut of an incomparable negligée, the princess talked on, and on...

It was the same divine impetuosity, the same eloquent ardour which had caused Rilke to flee from the Comtesse de Noailles,[1] '*as before a dangerous being*'. He had to respond to questions, pretexts for new confidences that had to be heard over again. A maid passed by, carrying breakfast on a tray. Freshly polished shoes vanished in the darkness, seized by a hand lacking an arm. Finally, Rilke managed to bring the conversation to a close. In his room he found his lunch now cooled and the pages of an interrupted letter that the wind had suddenly scattered about the table...

The nature of the relations that Rilke maintained with this part of Paris that we had nicknamed, with a Proustian term, 'in the environs of the princess', seems to me to emerge quite clearly from the memories that Miss Natalie Clifford-Barney reported in her *Aventures de l'Esprit*.[2] In a welling of sympathy, Rilke right away approached the 'Amazon' beloved of his friend Paul Valéry. But Miss Barney neglected to read the *Notebooks* that Rilke had sent her with a dedication full of deference: '*So I don't have to tell her... the rest.*' In vain does she then invite him to social gatherings, where he fears, he writes, '*not to be able to endure the ordeal of these divergent spirits and the winds of their atmospheres*'.

Rilke hesitates to indulge in the chances of this '*vague and inadequate crowd*' which threatens to become '*the symbol of my Parisian sojourn.*' The poet evades, the Amazon becomes irritated, weary. The opportunity, desired by the poet, for a '*calm and thoughtful evening*' '*in a small assembly*' does not present itself. The adventure is missed. It would be a long time after that Miss Barney would read Rilke's work and claim this heritage, with belated recognition. 'Why had we been, Rilke and I, too discreet, too absent or too clumsy?'

Other testimonies confirm the distress some contacts caused to Rilke, or the incomprehension he encountered in certain circles. Jacques Benoist-Méchin,[3] who noticed him for the first time at a Parisian salon, attests:

> from the first glance he caused me to feel, I must confess, an infinite pain… for everything appeared to wound him. The brightness of the chandeliers, the din of the overly lively conversations. He had appeared to emerge from the darkness of the depths, and his politeness only exacerbated my uneasiness towards him. By wrenching him out from the silence, it seemed to me that I was doing him an injustice, that I was committing an unnecessary act of cruelty towards him. I felt that each of my words caused him suffering, like those plants whose marvellous delicacy expands or contracts the leaves according to the most imperceptible nuances of light or shadow.

Even in those less eclectic atmospheres where one would presume to have more favourable exchanges, Rilke did not always find the audience which he needed.

Raymond Schwab,[4] who observed Rilke at the home of a Parisian author 'speaking in front of him, his eyes lost, head cocked to one side, and something in his whole bearing is bent, the nape of his neck, all the joints, and even that drooping moustache', describes the effect produced by Rilke's words:

> In this living room, where we began by forming a circle around him, little by little people discreetly took their leave, soon wearying of Rilke's loquacity, speaking directly out in front of him, explaining, without any regard to the effect produced, through what automatism his dream was translated into uncontrolled words when he switched from prose to verse, an activity in his eyes fundamentally at odds—I have never seen anyone underscore the difference to this degree, nor, my faith, move away from oneself with such swiftness, and, further, with carelessness, the listeners, by deducing over-generously things of far too great importance.
>
> After a matter of minutes, I remained his sole audience, myself, moreover, I admit, opposing by some silent scepticism this faith in automatism. I have no doubt [Raymond Schwab told me] that these same people are today Rilke fanatics one and all. But on that day—it must be said—they had judged him a bore.

But sometimes Rilke experienced joys at these Parisian evenings which stimulated him. This is how one morning he spoke to me of the Théâtre des Petits Comédiens de Bois,[5] who gave a series of studio performances and whom he had wanted to see again on several occasions since this spectacle had delighted and touched him: '*You have to go. It's an absolute must. It's a unique and wonderful thing,*' he enthused to me. Then he described these strangely personal puppets that Mme Julie Sazonova had brought back from Russia, Turkey and Italy and which she was trying to bring back to life in these studio scenes.

I went to see the *petits comédiens de bois* on whom Rilke had expounded to me at length. Mme Sazonova founded her marionette theatre in St Petersburg, but during the 1917 Revolution she emigrated and the wooden puppets, of which she owned a rare and unusual collection, slumbered for a long time in the base of her travelling trunks. Yet her taste for puppets remained as keen as ever, and during her travels in Turkey and Italy she had succeeded in obtaining the most curious specimens from Turkish and Italian marionette theatres and securing the support of a number of Italian puppet handlers, heirs of the traditions of the Commedia dell'arte. It was this collaboration between Russian and Italian artists which made it possible to organize the studio performance.

Puppets attracted Rilke for a good number of reasons. They were close to those 'things' he spoke of with such significative insistence and which moved him because, by dint of being involved in human life, they appropriate a subtle beauty and guard with strange perseverance the imprint of human gestures and feelings. Further, he loved the peculiar mannerisms and awkwardness of these dolls with names like Vania, Macha, Livia, Traccolo or Karagheuz, these peasants of the Russian village festival, drawn by Mme Gontcharova and the whole orchestra of woodwind musicians whose faces and gestures, controlled by the precise play of the wires, achieved a fantastic expressiveness.

Rilke had discovered this characteristic trait of puppets which struck all those who penetrated the universe of the *petits comédiens de bois*: we don't do with a puppet just what we want. Like dolls, like works of art, puppets were a step above mere objects.

Made by man in his likeness, they possessed a soul, curiously personal, sometimes welcoming to our desires, more often resistant to our games.

Once sculpted and dressed, the puppet has a personality and life of its own, which reserves surprises even for those who created it. It responds as it wishes to the calls of the handler, who appeals to it in a certain sense. When we wish to coerce it, it laughs or takes its revenge. Neither object nor being, it exists on a particular plane and makes use of its freedom by turns comical or fantastic.

The strange charm it exudes comes from this demon which seems to animate it and whose mischief will only appear little by little to those who were of the belief that they held it in their power.

This mysterious and personal life of the puppets fascinated Rilke in itself, as a game rich in surprises. But he went further: to the point of preferring these little wooden actors to the flesh-and-blood version. Rilke scarcely appreciated contemporary theatre, which to him appeared a *trompe-l'oeil* devoid of style or symbolic value. He blamed it for translating feelings of gross insufficiency, on a level of false generality. Save for rare exceptions, the actors irritated him by their impotence in giving themselves entirely to the work, by their facile realism, their tendency towards pretentious posing. Further, he was convinced that the path which led back to the purest and highest traditions of theatre passed through this little carpenter's bench of the old puppet theatre.

Beneath the face of the wooden doll, the characters of Shakespeare or Cervantes, Pergolesi or Aristophanes could regain their full meaning. The puppet—like the mask of ancient theatre—permitted the elimination of crude realism and the invasive personality of the actor. Rilke saw no other path open to the theatre than the symbolism of the Middle Ages or ancient tragedies. It was then a reflection of such concerns that he found in the ingenious and charming creations of these *petits comédiens de bois*, whose games confused traditions and images of Venice, Constantinople and Russia.

XI

LOU ANDREAS-SALOMÉ, GORKI, TOLSTOY

THE MEETING OF JULIE SAZONOVA and her group of Russian artists is not the only opportunity to revive Russian memories offered Rilke during his stay in Paris. These memories were so vivid in him that he had it in mind to write an account of his travels in Russia. In the same way that after the war he felt irresistibly drawn towards Paris until that desire had been satisfied, he sought to torment himself by reliving within the '*Russian miracle*' of his youth by resurrecting the episodes of his distant journeys of 1900 and 1901.

What would these memories of Russia have looked like if Rilke had found time to exhume them? The pages of the *Notebooks* on Nicolai Kousmitch and on the death of Gricha Otrepjoff,[1] the letter on the Easter celebrations in Moscow perhaps allow us to conjure a rough idea. The first of these episodes concerns a memory of a hotel neighbourhood in St Petersburg, to which the *New Poems* also allude; the second, inspired by a childhood reading, became clearer during the long hours that Rilke had spent at the Russian National Library, where he read mainly Russian historians, amongst others Karamzin, Solovieff etc.

LOU ANDRÉAS-SALOMÉ, GORKI, TOLSTOY

Since his great journey, Rilke had retained a particular tenderness for Russia that was sustained by readings and correspondence. His faithful friendship for Lou Andréas-Salomé, which never ebbed, even though he lost sight of this intelligent companion of his younger self for many years, rested on their common memories of Russia and the share that this great friend had taken from her Slavic *Erlebnis*.[2]

Although he had little opportunity to speak Russian and later he read certain Slavic authors in German or French versions, he still read this language fluently and we know that following his travels he translated a novel by Dostoyevsky, stories and plays by Chekhov, as well as poems by Drozhzhin.[3]

In Capri, Rilke approached Maxim Gorki during the period of his exile. Despite an initial mistrust of this Revolutionary, '*who celebrates himself as an anarchist, but who scatters around him—fortunately!—more money than bombs*', he spoke of him with intelligence. He did not place him in the same rank as Gogol, Tolstoy or Dostoyevsky and criticized him for judging art less as an artist than as a Revolutionary, but he ended feeling sympathy for this crude man, deeply rooted in the Russian land, and for his '*smile which traverses with such profound certitude all the sadness held in his face*'.

Over the months of his Parisian sojourn, Rilke took great pleasure in reading *Les Messieurs Golovleff* by Chtchédrine in the French translation I leant him.[4] He also read several works by Ivan Bunin of which he had been made aware.[5] His admiration for the *comédiens de bois* of Julie Sazonova did not ultimately stretch to the Russian marionettes—coachmen wrapped in their furs, peasant women in their *kokoshnik*,[6] rough and borrowed *moujiks*[7]—of which Mme Gontcharova had just designed the models.

The memories that Rilke had guarded of Russia can be demarcated, at least in a negative way, by two remarks.

Like many travellers coming from the West, Rilke had only known Russia in the spring and summer. Thus the images he evoked were never memories of snow, sleds or extreme cold, but on the contrary were impressions of abundance, fecundity, profusion, of immensity. Almost all the winter impressions found in the *Notebooks* relate to memories of Sweden or Bohemia. Of Russia, Rilke had retained especially that poetry which emerges from the infinitude of the Steppes, the strange impersonality of a country lacking any horizon, and this sense of human presences which had left his Slavic heart all aquiver.

The second particularity of the experience that Rilke had made of Russia is that of social problems; class conflicts appeared to have eluded his attention. He who in Paris had shuddered at the spectacle of human misery and had sought it out with an almost unhealthy insistence, had experienced nothing similar in Russia—or at least these impressions had been erased by others of greater power. He also showed little interest in those Russians engaged in the Revolutionary adventure.

There is in one of his letters from the time of his meeting with Gorki a curious passage which partly explains this distance. To his friend Karl von der Heydt, he wrote:

> *I think that the Revolutionary is the exact opposite of the Russian: in the sense that the Russian can be Revolutionary in much the same way a cambric handkerchief can be used to wipe off ink: at the cost of a total ignorance of its true qualities.*

On the other hand, Rilke, who felt in so many ways an exile of life, could only really be attracted by those White Russian enclaves of Paris whose existences of a fatalist and disenchanted Bohemia inspired him with a curiosity mixed with pity and tenderness.

The charm that Russia now exerted on him was linked to this notion of a deep and definitive burial of the country he had known. Russia was indeed his homeland, his homeland for all time, but in the sole domain of a memory whose reality had become forever inaccessible.

―――

Amongst the episodes of his Russian trip that I heard Rilke recount, there was one which had bestowed on him in a striking way this impression of the immensity of the Russian plain, which he readily recalled.

Rilke and his partner Lou Andréas-Salomé had disembarked at nightfall in some little country station, I don't recall which, from where a car was to take them to a neighbouring property. It was a beautiful summer night, and whilst the horses trotted along the track, Rilke and Lou Salomé at times contemplated the sky above studded with stars, and at others this limitless plain with its moving grasses and receding contours over which they travelled.

After a while Rilke and his friend were surprised to see a light in the distance in a direction in which, if the coachman were to be believed, no village existed for several hundred versts. The horses were still trotting on, but this mysterious light neither moved away nor drew closer. Its presence could not be explained, but it ended up becoming as natural in this rustling summer night as the glint of those thousands of stars in the heavens. It was only a few days later that Rilke and his friend were afforded the quite simple explanation: a fire had started several hundred versts away. Despite the vastness of the distance, it was the far-off glow of this fire which they had witnessed that night.

But the central episode, to which he always returned when he spoke of Russia, was his visit to Tolstoy, to Yasnaïa Polyana.[8] For my part, I heard him tell the story of his meeting twice over, each time with the details slightly different. Rilke had already met Tolstoy the previous year, in St Petersburg. But it was only following this first trip that he had become sufficiently familiar with Russian to read Tolstoy in the original. Furthermore, when in 1901 he left Moscow heading south, had he not possessed the ardent desire to see the great writer again, and savoured the idea of paying him a surprise visit at his estate, which Tolstoy continued to inhabit even though he had given all his other possessions to his wife and sons? It was as if the figure of Tolstoy would only assume its essential colour here, against the backdrop of a Russian spring, amongst the birches and laburnums of the park of Yasnaïa Polyana, the most powerful and moving vision of which Rilke had formerly received from the great writer himself.

Rilke and Lou Salomé arrived in Yasnaïa Polyana one morning in May. Along the way they had learnt by chance that the count had returned home. After being driven by automobile to the nearest village, they presented themselves at the entrance to the estate as modest pilgrims, such as were then arriving in large numbers to seek out the famous author of *War and Peace*. The two visitors, it appears, had bad luck. Tolstoy was in one of those increasingly frequent periods of exasperation during the course of which the antagonisms between his doctrines and the life he led—between his dreams of humility, of renunciation and the great surges of pride and sensuality which still harassed this septuagenarian—made him violent, aggressive, all but unapproachable. He received both visitors brusquely, scarcely maintaining a pretence of recognizing Lou Salomé, then abandoned them to their fate in the entrance hall of the house. For a time the eldest son of the count kept company with the two dispirited visitors, who had envisaged an altogether different kind of welcome.

However, they believed they could distinguish, in the smattering of words that Tolstoy had pronounced whilst withdrawing, the vague promise to receive them later in the day. Not wishing to be discouraged, Rilke and Lou Salomé took a stroll in the park and returned to the house around midday. They had barely entered the hall and were awaiting the luncheon invitation which, in this deserted countryside, would seem almost obligatory, when suddenly behind a glass door a violent discussion erupted. Another step and they were the midst of a domestic drama: it was Countess Tolstoy who was making a scene with her husband.

> *We waited a few moments, listening to these vociferations, and were on the point of leaving again, definitively disappointed, when the door opened and the countess appeared. At first she seemed taken aback finding us there, then, fixing us with a stern look, she asked us what we wanted. She was still a beautiful woman, with large dark eyes, whose voice bore almost a masculine timbre.*
>
> *'We are waiting for the count,' I said. 'My husband is suffering and will not be in a position to receive you'; she began turning away again with a certain abruptness. Fortunately, Lou Salomé had the presence of mind to declare that we had already seen Tolstoy earlier, and the countess, perhaps regretting her overly abrupt response, murmured a few words of apology. To regain composure, she selected some books from a shelf, then withdrew.*

Once more we were alone, the argument was intensifying by leaps and bounds. We recognized the voice of the countess, whose exclamations and sobs interrupted the angry voice of the count. Doors banged, the scene moved through the house, dragging, so it seemed, others into the uproar.

There were a few minutes of silence, then the door opened again and we saw Tolstoy appear. He seemed both fatigued and exasperated, his hands faintly trembling, but his gaze was absent. At first he didn't seem to recognize us and distractedly cast us a few questions without listening to the answers. In turn he withdrew.

On the other side of the wall we made out sounds of whispering, a tearful woman's voice, shaken by sobs, Tolstoy's now softened voice... the count reappeared. He held his cane in his hand. This time his gaze was entirely lucid and even strangely piercing beneath his bushy eyebrows. 'Would you care to have lunch with the others, or will you walk with me?' he questioned in a powerful voice where impatience and irony commingled.

Even if the welcome we received from the countess had been less daunting, our choice was already made in advance: naturally we preferred to walk. We set off together. Tolstoy walked beside us, with giant strides, talking prodigiously, as if to himself. We passed through the countryside, a landscape of grasslands and birches, of whose beauties he was familiar and where he finally seemed to become himself again. From time to time he would nibble on a piece of grass, or pluck a flower whose scent he inhaled and which he then a little later cast aside, random gestures with which he punctuated his words.

We conversed about many different things: of the surrounding landscape, of Russia, of God, of death... As he spoke Russian and expressed himself with vitality, I did not always grasp all his words. But all he said had an accent of elemental power, an air of strength and majesty.

Sometimes I looked sideways at this broad face with its high cheekbones, the enormous ears beneath white locks that the wind stirred, the dilated nostrils which inhaled the spring with a sort of sensuality. He strode on in his peasant blouse, long beard floating, sweeping gestures like those of a prophet, but the eye sharp and terribly present. It is this image of him which has stayed with me, and it counted for more than his words.

Naturally it would be necessary to give strength to Rilke's story, to find the movement of his words, all that contributed an attitude, a gesture, the way of insisting on certain words, a pause or a glance. After I expressed surprise that he had never felt the need to consolidate this memory, Rilke told me that he was thinking about it in precise terms. Now, had he then forgotten or was the following letter a little too thin compared with what he wished to write? He himself had once recounted, straight after his departure from Yasnaïa Polyana, his visit to Tolstoy, in a letter addressed to Sofia Nicolaevna Schill,[9] a letter which was found after her death. By comparing the account there with that which Rilke shared with me, we can appreciate the curious shift that time makes to such images. In any case Rilke's dominant impression remained the same. Time, far from weakening it, seemed to have reinforced it. Tolstoy had perhaps spoken to Rilke of death, of loneliness. But above all it is the memory of a spring overflowing with sap which he retained from this journey. To Sofia Schill he wrote:

Returning on foot to Kolowska, we relished this land of Tula, where poverty and wealth co-exist, not as opposites, but more like different words, most fraternal, an expression of one and the same life which fulfils itself in a hundred carefree and jubilant forms.

XII

RODIN, DE MAX, ISADORA DUNCAN

BETWEEN THE TWO extreme dates of 1904 and 1910 is located—with stops and starts, with temporary infidelities to Paris and returns of tenderness for this '*One place whose vast and generous hospitality always remains for me a homeland*'—the birth of *The Notebooks of Malte Laurids Brigge*. Begun in Rome, in a workshop in Strohl-Fern Park, Rilke traces the last chapters on the solid table of oak that Rodin had lent him for his study on the rue de Varenne, this table at which he sat saying: '*Look, this is the table of Rodin, I have to go further here than ever before.*' And in April 1910, when he left for Germany, he can finally take with him the papers of the young Dane, to deliver them to his publisher Kippenberg in Leipzig. To Countess zu Solms-Laubach[1] he wrote:

> *Malte Laurids Brigge gradually took on a shape completely detached from myself, acquiring its own existence and character and interested me all the greater the more it seemed something apart from myself. I don't know to what extent we can conclude from his papers that he can be said to possess an entire life. What this imaginary man experienced internally (through Paris and through his memories which are revitalized in Paris) has expanded in all directions; further notes would always be necessary, and what constitutes the book in no way forms a complete ensemble.*

> *It's rather like finding a drawer of papers in disorder, as if, for the moment at least, we shall find nothing more there and will have to be content with that. Without doubt, from an artistic point of view it is a rather parlous unity, but it is possible in human terms and what rises behind all this, in spite of all, is a sketch of existence and an intertwining of forces and shadows which are in motion...*

———

The Rilke of those years, 1908–1911, is the one we observe in the park of the Hôtel Biron where he would sometimes take an evening walk. Despite his desire to '*take everything up again from the beginning*', he is no longer the young man from rue Cassette or rue Toullier, timidly withdrawn in his solitude.

We may discern in the second volume of the *Notebooks* all that space found in the furthest corners of the Hôtel Biron park, 'that enchanting jumble of fruit tree, pasture and plants', that 'living tapestry', wrote Judith Cladel,[2]—which his travels in Provence and Italy opened up to his dreams. The arduous chores and material concerns that oppressed him at the time when, volunteer secretary to Rodin, he accepted his hospitality at Meudon were here spared him. Now he is the one who can invite his great friend into his home at the Hôtel Biron and, magnanimously setting aside the master's past injustices, reveal to Rodin this beautiful seventeenth-century residence and its reclaimed park, which will seduce the sculptor to the point that he himself will soon choose to set up his workshop there.

It is of this second period of his relationship with Rodin that Rilke expressed a preference, both because the memory was closer to him and because this free enclave had allowed him to judge the man and the artist with greater independence.

Their first encounter, two years the after the falling-out—a falling-out caused by a futile misunderstanding concerning a letter of whose content Rilke had for twenty-four hours neglected to inform Rodin—was simple and warm. On the basis of this new equanimity, Rodin confided to Rilke some of his despondencies as an artist and his intimate concerns.

Already in Meudon, Rilke had penetrated quite deeply into the intimate life of Rodin. Commensal and companion of the master, he, so sensitive, had virtually suffered from the heedlessness with which Rodin indulged his whims and abandoned himself to his exuberant temperament, dragging his entire entourage into his bouts of fury, his nervosity and outpourings of genius. But the huge admiration Rilke felt for Rodin expunged these false notes and the painful impression these tumultuous scenes caused him. On this subject Rilke related an anecdote which demonstrates in how charming a way he magnified Rodin's character by retaining incidents of which he witnessed only the most poetic aspect.

Mme Rodin, he recounted, was extremely jealous of the man who was only to become her husband towards the end of his life, and in truth there was good reason to be so. But in her apprehensions, the good Mme Rose[3] was not always guided by an infallible intuition. One day, when Rodin was off out early, without declaring the purpose of his walk and seeming in a particularly carefree mood, she became convinced that he was on his way to visit one of his mistresses and so she resolved to follow him. At the Gare Montparnasse the master buys a ticket for Chartres. Mme Rodin does likewise.

When Rodin descends to the platform she follows him, more and more convinced that she will soon know the secret of some new infidelity. Rodin leaves the station and continues on his journey, with the assured step of a man who knows exactly where he is heading. He finally stops on an esplanade lined with gardens from which you can take in the vast plain of La Beauce.[4] Looking up, Mme Rodin is obliged to face reality: Rodin had a rendezvous with Chartres cathedral!

At the Hôtel Biron, where Rilke was Rodin's neighbour for the turbulent period dominated by the Duchesse de Choiseul,[5] the discomfort was worse, but at least Rilke had regained his freedom and he was no longer closely involved in the day-to-day life of the master. Furthermore, he was able to judge him, pained to see him sink into error and ridicule. He was no longer solely the master whose presence aroused strengths and convictions; he was a man, unquestionably great, but who could still be wrong and whose faults were the price of his power.

If Rilke exclaimed in admiration at the bodies of women or Cambodian dancers that the master's pencil sensually sketched with such assuredness, he was no less convinced that Rodin had not really understood the true nature of woman, which is more elevated and more beautiful than that which dominates the minds of most men, the brief act of love.

They must have been the most curious conversations when Rilke spoke to Rodin of *La religieuse portugaise* or of Louise Labé,[6] when the sculptor celebrated woman as the veritable sap of his work, the intoxicating wine of his life. Having learnt much from Rodin by following his example, Rilke learnt even more from him by refuting his ideas, clarifying, as a reaction against Rodinian sensuality, this pure image of the 'loving one' that blossomed in the *Notebooks*.

During the period of disaccord with Rodin, Rilke found a powerful affection which already occupied an important place in his life, but which grew even stronger under the effect of the injustice he had suffered: the faithful friendship of Émile Verhaeren.[7]

I am not certain that the truth of the friendship between Rilke and Rodin can be simply reduced to a profound misunderstanding, such as are possible with men of this type, due to their imagination and the sheer mobility of their genius. (Didn't Rilke say that Rodin never paid little heed right up to the first word of his work?)

Whilst Rodin seems to have only rarely departed from his role as sacred 'pupil of God', and was blind to everything that did not concern himself and his art, Rilke continued to discover in Verhaeren a sympathy which extended to his own work and which, therefore, was a powerful reassurance.[8]

During his years in Paris he frequently paid visits to Verhaeren in his villa in Saint-Cloud, where he was welcomed with unswerving and faithful affection. His reading of Rembrandt and certain poems by Verhaeren were amongst the determining reasons for his trip to Belgium. On the other hand, he had found in *Les Villes tentaculaires* the feeling of oppression before the modern city that he himself had experienced on arrival in Paris.[9]

This poetic figure Rilke may well have idealized and modelled by the strength of his gratefulness. But he always spoke to me of the Belgian poet with fervent affection and an accent of sincerity which surely places this friendship amongst his most contented and serene experiences.

Amongst the tenants who occupied rooms on the various floors and outbuildings of the Hôtel Biron, which a judicial administrator managed following the law of separation and which were rented as separate apartments, there was still the actor Édouard de Max, Jean Cocteau, the painter Henri Matisse, Mme Clara Rilke-Westhoff, who was a sculptor and had been a student of Rodin, the Russian Youriévitch, etc.

In his *Portraits-souvenir* published in 1935, Cocteau prides himself on having preserved the gardens of the Hôtel Biron by alerting the press to the property developers who had their gaze firmly locked on to this seven-hectare park in the heart of Paris and offering a delegation of the 'Friends of the Louvre' the honours of his apartment. On the other hand, if memories are to be believed that Rilke retained from this period, Jean Cocteau was also one of those who provided—moreover involuntarily—ammunition for the opponents of this new affectation of the former residence of the Duchesse du Maine, for de Max and Cocteau were wont to organize noisy parties in the park and recurrent outbursts of the voices of their friends they assembled in their bachelor pads or beneath the lime trees in the courtyard often disturbed the poet's solitary nocturnal labours.

By having a bathroom installed in the sacristy of the ancient chapel of Les Dames du Sacré-Coeur, de Max achieved the distinction of having both the disinterested and interested defenders of the Hôtel Biron swiftly ranged against him, and the press campaign that followed forced the administrator to give notice to all the tenants.

Alongside a number of American or Slav women of letters or artists, Isadora Duncan had also hired, for her dance class rehearsals, a gallery in the Hôtel Biron, in the pavilion, now demolished, situated at the centre of the main courtyard. Residing in Neuilly and constantly drawn into a whirlwind of performance tours and sudden passions, she only made the rarest of appearances. Flitting from lover to lover, Isadora gathered the nectar of the male sex like a bee with translucent wings, heavy and fattened on the honey of pleasure, but so airy in spite of everything before her blue curtain with its capacious folds.

Isadora Duncan, possessed of the pride of motherhood, had around that time resolved to conceive a child by the greatest living poet, so this son she projected, like a movement in dance, might enjoin 'the power of the intellect' to the physical beauty which she prided herself on donating to him. To ensure that her selection would not alight on an unworthy suitor, she consulted the fashion designer Paul Poiret. He, who fortunately did not know Rilke, pronounced the name of Maurice Maeterlinck.[10] The author of *Pelléas et Mélisande* directly drew attention to his marital state and Poiret admits to not having the indiscretion to follow the scheme through to the end. Still, a few months later Isadora Duncan announced to her close friends that she would bear 'a beautiful tall child like this', indicating with her two hands exceptional dimensions.

Rilke at this time was content to admire from afar the dances of the bacchante who mimed Chopin like a paean and for whom the music seemed to release under her rhythmic step the intoxicating aroma of crushed grapes. Eleonora Duse, with her sensitive fragility, was of more appeal to him.[11] But he was as yet unaware of what danger these colourful neighbours in the Hôtel Biron had placed him in...

In January 1912, all the tenants, having received the order to leave, evacuated the premises, with the exception of Rodin, who refused to go and initiated a protracted struggle against the administration, until the State left him the old palace whose discovery he owed to Rilke, in exchange for the legacy of his works.

Rilke had already left the Hôtel Biron a few months earlier before the general exodus, seized by one of those sudden desires to travel which sometimes took hold of him. In the spacious garden by the boulevard des Invalides he vacillated between Spain, Egypt and Italy...

Then an invitation directed him temporarily towards Duino on the Adriatic coast, where the first of the *Elegies* were unexpectedly to be born.

XIII

ROSES, CATS AND DOGS

IN PARIS RILKE WANTED not so much to see the friends he had once known there, but more the numberless faces of the city, the changing aspects of the street. To take up these explorations once more, which twelve years of Parisian life had never exhausted, was one of his preferred pleasures.

The Île Saint-Louis, the Jardin des Plantes, Notre-Dame, the Luxembourg, the Tuileries—so many familiar landscapes with which he liked to surround himself. But there were also the more secret corners that he discovered or sought out again; the Square du Vert-Galant at the most western point of the Île de la Cité, the Place des Vosges, or the little garden of the church of Saint-Julien-le-Pauvre where he happily lingered after attending the Armenian service.

Just as in Venice he flattered himself that he could, like an authentic native, cross great distances without the assistance of gondolas, taking to secret alleyways and innumerable interior passageways which allowed one to travel almost the entire city on foot, likewise he recalled with amusing pride that he had victoriously endured the Parisian geography exam invented by Valery Larbaud,[1] which included a certain number of difficult questions, such as listing the principal squares of Paris that contained fig trees and giving as accurate a date as possible of their flowering.

Rilke spoke of these things with a lightness that betrayed the importance he attached to them. It was during his walks that he had come across the night shelter on rue Saint-Jacques, the young girls who practise drawing at the Musée de Cluny, where the unicorn of the tapestries from the Château de Boussac continues to reflect its face in the mirror circled in white on a rose background of infinite tenderness, or the motionless man who threw breadcrumbs to the birds of the Luxembourg, the children's carrousel, with its white elephant and its yellow lion baring its fangs, and even the strange paralytic who even as night fell was dragging himself along past the gate of the Luxembourg.

Out of this astonishing quest for the life of another time emanated sadness, fear, but sometimes also joy.

One morning Rilke arrived at our apartment bearing a magnificent spray of red roses. They were intended for my wife, who was then suffering from a protracted illness and who on occasion sometimes accompanied us at our reading hour, reclined on a couch, at the rear of the room where we worked.

As I reproached Rilke for spoiling my wife, he recounted to me the following. Earlier, at the corner of boulevard Saint-Michel, he had stopped in front of the florist's stand to choose some roses:

The florist was kneeling somewhere amidst the profusion of stems and greenery. She got up and came over to me. Then, all of a sudden, I recognized her. It was her, it was really her: the young florist who would hum a tune behind her stall twenty years ago, when I first came to Paris. It was the same tanned face, the same slightly mischievous look, the same curly black hair. She wore a scarf tied about her neck, which in the chill of morning highlighted the red of her lips and the freshness of her complexion. And she was wearing thick wool stockings and ankle socks like those worn by Ticino peasant women. It was her, there could be no question. And as youthful-looking as twenty years ago!

Rilke's joy had been so great that he could not help but buy all the roses the young florist had on her stall, and it was this spray, heavy and fragrant, that he had just placed on the couch beside my wife. We had accepted the miracle as a gracious pretext, a friendly game courtesy of Rilke's imagination. However, the florist, we were to learn later, was quite simply the daughter of the one Rilke had known before the war and it just so happened there was a striking resemblance between the two women. But what does it matter, in the end, such a detail? Even if the florist had been someone else, would Rilke not have wished any less to recognize this face from times past that he so needed to recapture. In any case, the roses had not changed. Who, indeed, could distinguish the roses of one season from those of another?

Into that spray of roses which littered the couch our young cat came that morning to play; he would introduce himself by passing through the open window of the balcony, then turn and twist about us as we worked.

Rilke stroked his charged fur as he passed, in the same way he caressed Edmond Jaloux's cat on the rue de Valois, a beautiful Siamese named Racoon, who, weary of living amongst the books and parakeets, between Venetian chests and green lacquerware of

China, sometimes clung on to his master's visitors or rolled at their feet, galvanized by strange new odours from the outside world.

We told Rilke the story of our cat, Mousse, nicknamed 'The Angora of the South'. My wife had wanted a cat for a long time when a friend from Avignon offered to send us a newborn kitten. The mother must have been a magnificent angora. This friend described her fur to us, spoke of her intelligence and feline suppleness. With a little patience, soon we too would have our own angora.

Finally, a letter informed us that our young cat had been entrusted to the care of a commission agent at Avignon train station who would deliver it to our home. A box duly arrived in which we found, amidst a thin layer of wet sawdust, a tiny meowing creature, bathed in sweat, face to face with a huge pile of poo. Alas! The journey to Paris had transformed the Avignon angora into a humble street cat, and despite the optimistic outlook of our Provençal friends his fur never chose to grow.

Rilke laughed whilst hearing this story, as he sometimes knew how to laugh, in an almost guttural voice, his eyelids pursed into little creases, his head shaken by nods. In turn, he spoke of the young cat of Balthus, the son of Baladine Klossowska, which he had with him in Geneva and of whose heartbreaking adventure he had commented in the preface to an illustrated album which is one of the rare French texts in prose we have by his hand.[2]

Rilke had some experience with cats and liked them, although he claimed to have been never able to quite convince himself that they really existed. He admired the way they seemed to drop into our world, as if from the sky, to knock over an inkwell or entangle a ball of wool, then, with a sudden leap, to escape once more as if we were only a projection of our mind, a shadow that their pupils would not register. This independence of cats seemed to him a virtue because it allowed him to accommodate their almost imaginary presence, which weighed no more than a phantom.

With dogs it was altogether quite different, he said; excessively humanized, dogs were the result of a kind of pact between man and animal. In their faithful and fearful look, with their muzzle moist and begging, man existed with such power, with virtues so exaggerated, that the constraint exerted on us by this look could become insupportable.

So Rilke always tended to avoid dogs, or took great care to maintain a sufficient distance between them and himself to ensure that no dog conceived of directing one of these ardent and servile admiring looks towards him with the risk of enchaining one to the other.

Since witnessing Lou Andreas-Salomé's little dog die, he had sensed a silent reproach in the animal's eyes towards his mistress—an episode recalled in a passage of the *Notebooks*—yet for all this he was still doubtless capable of petting a beautiful greyhound, or giving a piece of sugar to a basset hound who once visited him, and he even admired the tireless devotion of a shepherd's dog, though he had refused to welcome into Muzot the canine guardian that his friends had wanted to give him as a companion in his solitude.

And the ironic lightness of his words did not deceive as to his true feelings, when he told of the encounter he had one day with a stray dog who had wished to elect him master:

Neither quite man nor animal, the touching and pitiful half-caste dog is infinitely attracted to our world of relationships, but is unable to navigate it without our active assistance. He has lost this lack of concern, this yawning depth of instinct that we find in the eyes of an animal which is free. How many cats are justified in their disdain for the dog, they who have never deigned to take leave of their universe of cats!

The dog may sometimes reap the reward of his ceaseless adoration, under the caresses of a mistress who is suffering, or upon the body of a dead master whose hand he persists in licking. So perhaps his eyes take on that almost human expression of the lion on the tapestry of the Lady and the Unicorn at Cluny, and he accedes for an instant to this too-onerous existence which man trains him for mercilessly and without remorse. But almost immediately, feeling that they have somehow ceased to be dogs, they refuse all food, and they are found dead, a few days later, beside a grave or at the rear of their kennel, poisoned by human pride.

XIV

BETTINA VON ARNIM, LINA POLETTI AND ELEONORA DUSE

S PRING HAD MADE its entrance whilst we were reading *The Notebooks of Malte Laurids Brigge*, but Rilke could not enjoy it as he would have liked because he fell ill. One morning a brief note announced to me that, being indisposed, he could not attend our session. The following week having passed without his recovery, I decided to go and check on him. A few days later he wrote to me:

I have been terribly late in thanking you for your attentive visit; but if only authentically 'sick' and bedridden for a week or so, this flu, apparently lenient, left me in such a state of confusion and weakness that this whole period was for me one of loss and modest patience; I exposed myself to the sun (a rare thing, moreover, and unwise, but I was unable to see my friends and even more incapable of any mental effort).

I now hope to be able next week to resume the most agreeable hours of our shared work and I envision that then we will make great strides, wonderfully cadenced and concerted…

For some time now we had been discussing the second volume of the *Notebooks* and now were about to encounter on our path the visage of Abelone. First it was that chapter which describes the fever of reading which gripped Malte during the summer he spends with the young girl, then the episode of the letters from Bettina von Arnim that Abelone snatches from the young man's hands to read herself, out loud, with an emotion which betrays her own feelings.

Rilke asked me if I had read Arnim's *Goethes Briefwechsel mit einem Kinde*[1] and I had to admit I hadn't. I only knew of Bettina von Arnim from what little the history books say on the matter and what I had learnt from the pages of the *Notebooks* which transformed Goethe's young correspondent into an almost mythical being: the misunderstood lover whose power to love surpassed all.

> *For this strange Bettina, has, through all her letters, created space, a world of expanded dimensions. From the start it has spread through everything as if she had already overtaken her death. Everywhere she had settled deeply into being she became a part of it, and everything that happened to her was for all eternity contained in nature; there she recognized herself, she broke from it almost painfully; little by little she perceived, as if returning to tradition, how she called herself forth like a spirit and came face to face with herself.*
>
> *A moment ago, Bettina, you were still there; I understand. Is the earth now warm with you, and the birds do they not leave space for your voice? The dew is no longer the same, but the stars are still the stars of your nights. Where is the whole world not yours? How many times have you set it on fire with your love, and seen it blaze up and consume itself, in secret, replaced by another world, whilst all were sleeping...*

Now here was a surprise, for Rilke began to paint an altogether different Bettina from the one I had encountered in the *Notebooks*. Here was a young dizzy woman of superior intelligence who perched herself on the knees of maturing gentlemen, who launched herself at the faces of great men, who poked fun at Wieland and who had sworn to throw Goethe into a panic. Bettina, I had read in the *Notebooks*, had virtually erased Abelone, only borrowing her features to appear more alive in the eyes of Malte. But here's the thing: in the mind of Rilke, Abelone seemed to have exacted revenge by dissolving this magnificent image of she who preceded her. Bettina Brentano was nothing more than an impulsive young person in whom a surfeit of malice was combined with the exaltations of a *Backfisch*.[2] At the same time that her adventure with Goethe had been reduced to the proportions of an overly calculated idyll, the image of Goethe had grown once more. Rilke admitted that perhaps he had been a little unfair to the grand old man of Weimar and that, in his sovereign wisdom, he had undoubtedly had reason to resist the influence of the impetuous child.

He confessed to having ignored Goethe for a long time, but added that he had moved closer to him as he had more keenly felt the price and the potency of old age: '*When we are young we understand nothing,*' he said, perhaps thinking of that Prague era of which he could never speak about without a certain tension. '*Life is only a long apprenticeship.*'

Always the woman who loves surpasses the man who is loved, because life is greater than fate. Her gift of herself can be infinite; that is her happiness. But the nameless grief of her love has always been this: that they demand of her to limit this gift...

we read in the *Notebooks*.³ But Goethe had in his own way granted life and destiny, and this wise equilibrium should not be contested. Bettina was just a letter of the alphabet with which he had composed his work and this work was great and human, with a power that could stand up to life.

No, Bettina was no longer, in Rilke's eyes, the purest image of the loving woman. But other women's faces continued to present this myth, white and clear. And little by little one of them drew nearer to us, out of the dense sheaf of the *Notebooks*, a face that Rilke himself had known, loved; it belonged to Eleonora Duse.

It is difficult to reproduce that mixture of humour and emotion which often lent such a distinctive accent to Rilke's words, and rightly he focused on those subjects that moved him most. Perhaps this was the form that his modesty took in our familiar conversations. He started with telling me a few anecdotes about la Duse, only risking here and there a word of description, as if he were speaking of some rare and fragile bird.

For so quivering was this acute sensibility of Eleonora Duse that the slightest incident affected her to the extent of making her ill, and thus her company imposed a strain on the nerves of her companions which in the long term proved gruelling. Rilke recounted this walk he made with her, so uncongenially disturbed by the screech of a peacock, that Princess von Thurn und Taxis also cited in her memoirs. On a beautiful day, Eleonora Duse and her friend Mme X… (Lina Poletti),⁴ accepting Rilke's invitation, had undertaken an excursion to the islands.

The weather was radiant; settled on the grass, the friends were chatting amiably when a peacock suddenly approached them, sending out its shrill and hoarse cry, which naturally made them all start. But what for the others had been only a momentary upset was a massive shock for Eleonora Duse, a terrible emotion. Trembling in all her limbs and at the same time overcome by a tremendous fury, she vowed to flee the cursed place and demanded that we all leave right away. Their walk was suddenly over, misspent. A despondent Rilke was obliged to accompany his over-sensitive friend to her home, for she had not yet recovered from her seizure.

Such incidents were not uncommon. Another time, the buzzing of a fly, caught between the white tulle curtains which softened the light in Eleonora Duse's apartment, provoked a similar crisis. Everyone started searching for the fly, but then it abruptly stopped buzzing and could not be found. Barely had we sat down again and resumed our conversation when from the rather shadowy corner of the room the fly could be heard once more. This time Eleonora Duse was so exasperated she was near fainting, and she ended up fleeing, abandoning her guests, ceding her place to the fly, which she conceived as some gigantic spider, blotting out the entire sky.

In these scenes, as Rilke reported them, the comedic never ceased to border on tragedy, and it fused so intimately these two elements that it would have been very difficult for us to decide which one had lent its own impression. What Rilke admired most in la Duse was this power of a veritably dramatic temperament which could expand immeasurably, as if for the perspective of some vast amphitheatre, from the faintest movements of sensitivity.

The apparent disproportion between these incidents and the significance that they assumed in the life of la Duse demonstrated only this: that she was an actress to the marrow of her bones, that she lived perpetually on the plane of the dramatic and had to live there all the more violently since she believed herself by then to have finally renounced the stage.

But behind the actress and the anecdotes that portrayed her, little by little, the true image of la Duse to which Rilke subscribed, the image of the beating heart, of an infinitely sensitive woman, infinitely good, that life had dealt a cruel blow. It has been said that in the misanthropy and fiercely willed isolation of Eleonora Duse there was evidence of the artist's spite, or irritation caused by material difficulties which were largely the consequence of her own caprices. Rilke, who met la Duse in 1910, was convinced that she was nothing of the sort. It was his belief that the wound of love was the true explanation of this withdrawal at the height of her glory. Gabriele D'Annunzio,[5] he assured me, had acted towards la Duse with a terrible hardness, and despite the years that had passed she was still suffering the consequences of this injury.

In her despair, Eleonora Duse clung to an Italian woman of letters, Mme X… who was without doubt devoted but whom Rilke judged too simple, not delicate enough, and thus incapable of curing la Duse of her malaise. Eleonora Duse, however, was making efforts on her own, entering into a state of self-hypnosis around drama projects with her friend, whose writing gifts she overestimated, imagining her triumphant return as performer of these pieces written expressly for her. But these unrealizable hopes only implicated the great artist in an entanglement of sentimental obligations, bonds of recognition and imaginary duties, so much so that even her most disinterested friends yearned for the collapse of this hopeless friendship.

For months Rilke dwelt amidst the clubbiness of these two women; taking his meals almost daily with la Duse, sometimes witnessing sporadic quarrels between the two friends, sensing the mounting crisis of Eleonora Duse, seeking in vain to relieve her. In the end he felt so unsettled by this depressing atmosphere that he left for Venice, not long before Eleonora Duse herself severed her relations with Mme X. Although he continued from time to time to correspond with her, he was never to see his great friend again.

It was almost in the midst of these conversations that news came of the death of Eleonora Duse, during a tour of America. Rilke seemed distressed not only by this news, which revived his regret at having avoided the opportunity to see la Duse again in Venice in 1919, but moreover that the death of the tender interpreter of *Nora* and *La Dame de la mer*[6] had occurred in such barbaric conditions. He told me:

You had to have known Eleonora Duse to appreciate her acute sensitivity to the tiniest details of existence, you have to know how terrified she was of departures, of tours in far-off places, countries that were not the mirror of her soul, or simply strangers, to divine how much she must have suffered to be dying in some indifferent city in that America she so detested. Baltimore, Washington, Pittsburgh, loathsome names beside that dear Chioggia, the beloved hill of Asolo to which she remained so faithfully attached. What must she have endured, during the final weeks of her life, spending entire days on trains—she who had an innate horror of them—having to put up with the impresarios she couldn't bear, constantly shunted from palace to palace and having to endure that hostile climate; dust, din, foreign faces, rain, fog, all of it, and then finally to die in the room of some nondescript hotel,[7] what a sickening final chapter for her and what regrets for those who loved her and could do nothing to prevent this! A dreadful demise, sought by a destiny which, right to the end, never consented to relinquish that embrace from which she was already suffering when I first met her in Venice, now almost fifteen years ago. Yes, Eleonora Duse had her own death!

XV

GIRAUDOUX, GIDE, MAX PICARD

To write these memories, I am forced at moments to impose an artificial order on what in reality was bestowed upon me, in accordance with our readings, through digressions and moments of repose. Attempting to string together these remarks, I risk losing those which, scattered through our discussions, only took on a certain importance through comparison, or because Rilke repeated them in different forms and circumstances.

There was for example his interest in contemporary French letters. Many questions or allusions betrayed his astute knowledge of them, how deeply they attracted him. Not only had he loved Proust from day one, but he also read the works of the young post-war writers. He divined in these books an upsurge of lifeblood, a nascent force which to him seemed to authorize the highest expectations. For these young writers affected by the war, who expressed with a bitter violence their experiences, he felt a profound sympathy.

Generally speaking, he did not harbour that grandiose disdain so many great writers exhibit as they gain in age and glory, those who end up knowing only themselves. Although his readings were naturally matched to his own preoccupations and his state of mind at a given time—so that works had to wait for many months for that hour when they would suddenly be relevant—he read avidly and his choice was always eclectic.

During the months of his sojourn in Paris in the first half of 1925, he read indiscriminately Giraudoux, Colette, Chtchédrine, Ramuz, Aragon, Emmanuel Bove, Supervielle, Alain-Fournier, depending on his mood in the moment. However distant from him she might appear, in Colette he savoured the fire of the senses and that natural freshness found in her spontaneous images. As for Giraudoux, he considered him one of our strongest writers, yet at the same time reproaching him for not being fully aware of his highest qualities and sometimes losing his way in gratuitous frivolity.

One day, having come upon a copy of *L'École des indifférents*,[1] he leafed through it hurriedly and read me the beginning of the chapter *Jacques l'égoiste*.

> Death? The dead? I carry a thousand bereavements which do not even belong to me. Young people, young women, that I met once or twice and whose death I suddenly learnt of, appear to me and become my familiars. I dream almost continuously of them. Often it is Laure de Bergtill who leans over me and who is silent. Often it is Édith Gocelan, who succumbed after just three months of marriage. Resting against the wall, she too has no idea what to say. I question her:—Édith, is life still where you are?
>
> She takes my hand and presses it against her chest. Her heart is still there. But it does not beat with sharp and murderous blows, like our heart, a perfidious battering ram that undermines the fortress from within. Édith's heart is on fire. No veins, no arteries. An even heat fills her body. Her flesh is one like the flesh of fruits.

—And your hands Édith? I was told that the fingers of the dead are fused and their legs are no longer separated.

She smiles, crosses my fingers in her slender and distinct fingers, but she doesn't move.

—Is everything different where you live, Édith?

By way of response, the dead close their eyes.

—Everything is the same. Except that we have sovereign command over all things which, to you, are suspicious. The birds, patches of sun allow themselves to be caught. Our shadow does not revolve around us like a compass that measures life. It is always the length of our body, it never precedes us. And what people say about asphodels[2] is true; the meadows are sown with them, like cowslips.

—Do you pick them?

—We do not stoop, we always proceed standing upright.

—Édith! Édith, so it's true them? Your ankles, your knees are welded together?

She leans against my shoulder, sobs and I passionately console her. Tearing herself from my arms, she sinks, still upright, on to the wall; now only her hand passes the wall hanging, I kiss it, but it's to leave a caress on the hand of someone foundering. And I awake with a strange sadness, as if I discovered one day in my hand, having dreamt of India, a living Bengali…

Rilke closed the book.

Is that not a marvel that page? But why did he wander off there? Ah! If only Giraudoux realized that Édith was showing him the path to true poetry!

Rilke didn't only read books, journals also interested him and he preferred the most recent, the least known. This incessant flowering of ephemeral notebooks to poetry, to art, seemed to him one of the surest guarantors of French vitality and he browsed these chapbooks with a curiosity which was often richly rewarded. The verses he discovered in this way he carefully transcribed into his notebook, also noting the names of the poets who had made an impression on him and whom he wanted to know more about. Sometimes, when he arrived at my apartment, he would quote me one of his recent discoveries, such as those beautiful lines from the young Belgian poet Odilon-Jean Périer, who died not long after he penned them, aged only twenty-five:[3]

> Beautiful day, sober and deep like wild marble,
> that your corners of gold have lent me help,
> so much perfection makes one love his work,
> so much clarity distracts from love...

When Rilke was asked about his preferred contemporary Germans he was more hesitant. Hofmannsthal, Stefan George and Franz Werfel were the names he cited first. Further he named two women, barely known in France, Regina Ullmann and Ruth Schaumann,[4] whose poetry seemed significant to him. But he hastened to add that his knowledge was insufficient as to the production of recent years, and furthermore that he had no vocation for criticism and his role was neither to classify nor to judge. He admitted,

I harbour a deep distrust with regard to the whole abstract domain of aesthetic and literary deductions. Such judgements and comparison, as soon as they claim to take on a general character, so easily draw away from reality. They are in any case unimportant with regard to the need that I

may have, on a given day or at a certain moment, from a book or a poem and of the interior enrichment that I will owe them...

Indifferent to criticism of himself or others, Rilke nevertheless felt driven to express and communicate to those around him the enthusiasm that certain readings aroused in him. He was thrilled by a poetic success without any ulterior motive. He was no less generous in being devoid of that unconscious jealousy of which Paul Valéry said the most authentic artist is subject to, in the face of the perfection of a work that he himself did not create.

Rilke lived in the present of his heart, in the absolute of his emotion. Literary criticism was not to his taste. Willingly would he have transposed the world of Dostoyevsky:

It is a mistake to judge man as you do. There is no tenderness in you; there is only the feeling of severe justice; so you are being unjust.

―――

Rilke reserved all severity for himself and for that which touched him intimately, namely the translation of his works. In matters of translation he could reveal an unyielding rigour. If the versions of his poems which have appeared in France during his lifetime are so thin on the ground—compared to what transpired after his death—it was because he was at no great pains to authorize the publication of insufficient or too-approximate interpretations of his work and was loath to let his oeuvre become fragmented. As for *The Book of Hours*, the *Duino Elegies* and the *Sonnets to Orpheus*, he held that they were not collections of poetry but symphonic poems whose parts were powerfully linked and that one could not just divide them up without betraying the whole. As for the *Cornet*—which Gide had once declared an interest in translating—Rilke rejected more than a dozen contending versions before deciding just a few months before his death and, since Gide had definitively abandoned his project, to authorize the transcription by Suzanne Kra.

Rilke demanded that a translation fulfil two conditions: it was necessary that it be strictly and meticulously consistent with the original text; and secondly that it restores the movement of thought, the vital momentum of the line. Demands which appear somewhat contradictory! The whole artistry of the translator is however bound up with their reconciliation.

In the case of poetry, Rilke's demands were still more severe. Here the movement was rhythm, rhyme, music of the verse… a word-for-word translation, however conscientiously created it might be, which does not consider this crucial element was in his eyes an entirely futile exercise. It was to substitute a living body with a wax effigy, a petrified corpse. It was to take the work back to a secondary plane of analysis, of explanation, from which he always deliberately veered away from. It was better to abstain. I recall when Rilke recounted to me the irritation he had one day experienced concerning the translation that a writer—who was moreover one of his friends—had, without consultation, published in a magazine and which transposed into ornate and sparkling prose some pieces from *The Book of Images* and the *New Poems*. Undoubtedly Rilke knew better than anyone the extent of obstacles that the French language, by the fixity of relationships it establishes between words, through its overly abstract vocabulary, by the particularities of its rhythm, by the automatic sequence and logic of its constructions, set up in opposition to such an enterprise.

His poetic work still awaits the poet of genius who will render him the service that he himself rendered to Paul Valéry.[5]

Do you know le Dernier Homme *by Max Picard?*[6] [Rilke asked me one morning]. *I just saw that they've just published a French translation. It's an extraordinary book and quite terrifying. I am not sure if I should even urge you to read it.*

Before I was able to obtain a copy, Rilke had taken it upon himself to send me one. He discussed it with me a few days later.

He had known the author—of Austrian origin—in Lugano, and described him as a nervous little man with a prodigious vivacity. With an almost frenzied ardour, Max Picard had endeavoured to evoke, in his own way, this 'last man', of whom Nietzsche speaks in *Zarathustra*.[7] A man more and more depersonalized, whom the machine robs of meaning and physical form.

The being that Picard imagines and describes in a series of parables is no longer a man save by inertia or force of habit. He is not complete as man once was, but tries at most to merely offer a pretence. Soon he will no longer have a face at all and the animals will take fear before him. His presence disturbs or destroys even inanimate things. In truth, man has long since ceased to be. But the phantom who took his place is afraid of dying, he can't even manage to disappear. 'We fear that from the void, where one amongst them would be missing, something terrible would burst in.'

And Max Picard poses this question: 'Man has perished... so then, do we survive?'

Rilke, to whom the domain of anxiety was a familiarly trodden one, had been pinioned in the violent clutches of this philosophical nightmare by the monotonous and increasingly deranged swirling of images in this strange book. It was a condemnation of progress, a terrifying and mournful illustration of the idea of decadence.

Rilke, who in the *Sonnets to Orpheus* wrote that, despite the threat of the machine against the mind, our life, a play of pure forces, remains enchanted music for all those who wish to listen to it and wish to turn away from this strident and cruel dream. But the 'last man' had brushed against him with his face shorn of eyes or ears, and he could no longer prevent a measure of the anguish of this vision from remaining mixed into his freeborn dreams...

XVI

SPAIN, PROVENCE, VENICE

It was almost summer now. Rilke lingered longer in the Luxembourg, and when he arrived at our home the golden season and the morning garden still beckoned him to the balcony. '*How unique, how incomparable this Paris sky was*', he exclaimed. '*What subtle life, its generous variety lent to this landscape of such authentic intelligence!*'

We felt him lifted towards the welcome of the vast sky, this sublime garden, and all around the crowd of chimneys animated it with human presences like the sounding pipes of some immense organ.

On these mornings which encouraged more strolling than work, Rilke spoke openly of his travels, finding within him, in order to evoke them, images of Scandinavian apple trees, of a Danish or Italian springtime. During these conversations, he admitted to me on a number of occasions that after a few unfortunate attempts he had definitively given up travelling beyond the borders of Europe. Such far-flung journeys involved a depletion of strength which he now could not afford. Europe—its cities, its castles, its cemeteries, its museums and its libraries—seemed to him to be a vast enough terrain to occupy a single man's life. The plateau of this spiritual continent was for him Russia, Denmark and France. Germany, Austria and Italy only came later, as complementary colours which occupied a sort of middle ground between the choice atmospheres. Of Prague, the city of his youth, he spoke with some humour, reflecting doubtless unconsciously the grudge that he held against the young René Rilke who had formerly fallen for the allures of a pretentious bohemia. From his own notion of Europe, Rilke would have gladly severed England, a country with which he had only experienced disaccord and an unsatisfying relationship.

What was there for him anyway beyond Europe? The rare attempts he made to leave it—his travels in Algeria, Tunisia and Egypt—had been defeats in both the physical and moral sense. He was convinced that he had come up against the very boundaries of his being. Africa and Asia were great mysteries that he resigned himself to leaving aside intact, for fear of being forced to take on a task beyond his capabilities and strengths. For with countries, just as with men and books, he held that we do not have the right to do things by half and we should not undertake anything without having the will to go the whole distance.

As for America, it appeared to him impenetrable. One of his closest friends, Rudolf Kassner, once wrote that superlatives are contemptible because they rarely express a genuine figure and that they are most often merely a caricature. In Rilke's eyes, America was a human form of the superlative; for him it meant a total void.

In this moral continent, on which he had established a foothold and intended to remain, the lines of force which he obeyed were not, moreover, traced in an immutable and definitive manner. Spain, which for a long time had only appeared to him in certain dreams, like that Toledo of Greco torn by the storm, about which he had spoken to Rodin, had only emerged lately from long-overlooked depths. And Switzerland occupied a place apart, the peaceful landscape of his later years, to which he had ascribed a tenderness formed from recognition and friendship.

Towards the end of his stay in Paris, I believe that, under the influence of Valéry, he felt more and more attracted to the Mediterranean landscape and its harmonious civilization. He harboured a special nostalgia for Provence and was minded to leave Muzot, at least for the winter, to settle either around Avignon or in the region of Toulon. One morning Rilke brought me some old prints that he had purchased from the booksellers on the *quais* and which represented the valley of the Rhône in the region of Sierre and Sion. With their hills and towers, they were landscapes with strong, rounded contours, there was a romantic exuberance about them which left nothing to divine from the lofty double walls of rock which must have enclosed them.

In this valley Rilke assured me that many things—lines, colour, plants, light—reminded him of the Spain of Ronda, and it seemed to him that, as he descended the course of the river all the way to Provence, he would succeed in perfecting this resemblance without needing to deviate from the Rhône.

His intention was so firm to sojourn over the winter in Provence or on the Mediterranean coast—for fear of the harsh climate which confined him to his tower during the winter months—that he had begun to solicit information about potential places to stay.

It was in this frame of mind that he spoke to me about journeys— always too rushed for his liking—that he had made previously in the South of France. He knew well Arles, Orange, Avignon, Saint-Rémy-de-Provence, had visited their monuments and their museums, not forgetting those little sunny courtyards, half-cloisters, half-cemeteries, where one could find, he said, better than before any display case, the atmosphere of the times and the sense of reliving them. That lofty figures of this country were familiar to him, such as the medieval King René, of whom he spoke with predilection, and a memorial to whose life he had been thrilled to find in the church of Saintes-Maries-de-la-Mer, where he had witnessed over the course of a night the mysterious pilgrimage, half-gypsy, half-Provençal, half-Pagan, half-Christian, at the edge of the vast, windswept Camargue.[1]

But the Provençal landscape he proclaimed longest and with the deepest emotion was that petrified plateau of Les Baux, where a handful of shepherds, amongst tombs and rocky outcrops, appeared to be the last survivors of a proud race that once reigned there over several centuries, dominating the highways of France and Italy, over a flourishing city and country. The vast arena where Rome, Gaul and the Renaissance had superimposed their stones and tombs.

Rilke had wandered amongst these ruins, on this path which seemed to lead back to the past, but stopped short, as if cut off forever, at the edge of a verdant abyss. He walked over this immense terrace, with its gentle slope, where the rain of centuries had collected, and he lost himself in the rocky chaos where only a scattering of sheep were bleating. Tombs and ashes, rocks and capitals, together with the light of the Midi composed a setting where he could evoke the proud lineage of King René and the Counts of Baux, who wore on their shields the star with the sixteen rays of the wise men, which in his eyes represented a human image of the most magnificent splendour.

We were turning the last pages of the *Notebooks*. As if by chance they opened on to the same lands as the prodigal child traversed during his interminable wanderings.

SPAIN, PROVENCE, VENICE

Les Baux, the Alyscamps, Orange—it was as if Rilke had, before closing the book, sown here and there these enchanted words behind which rose up vast landscapes where he had always expected to return sooner or later. Would he pronounce them one day, these watchwords, which he had somehow kept in reserve in these final chapters of the *Notebooks*? He pondered.

Just as Muzot closed the cycle of the *Elegies*, Provence concealed, in his mind, words and images which had had time to mature since 1909 and which would unfold, soon perhaps, in some new combination. Those things which had only been gestured to in the *Notebooks* would form its powerful backdrop. It was a work in prose that he was thinking about, a book that could be to the *Duino Elegies*—he explained, responding to my questions, not without surmounting interior obstacles—what the *Notebooks* had been to the *New Poems* and *The Book of Images*.

But before I had succeeded in provoking these reluctant confidences we had stopped off again in Italy, and we met Abelone again in Venice.

We recalled the young Dane whom Malte meets in a Venetian salon during a social reception, who sings an unknown German song with a simplicity so perfect that it makes him think of Abelone. I had been held up for some time by these stanzas and by the challenge of rendering, as Rilke desired, the interior movement, the rhythm and, as much as possible, even the rhyme. My version in its provisional state had hardly satisfied either of us and it was understood that we would return to it later. In the meantime, Rilke spoke to me of Venice, about the powerful and hard reality of this city that he saw with different eyes than the majority of romantics who had sung about it. It was a crystal, he explained, a product of the persevering will of those who had drawn this marvel out from nothingness, from lagoons and swamps. The city he knew and loved had nothing languid or nostalgic about it. This was not the '*soft and opiate Venice of prejudices*' where some seek only the '*easeful lucrative swooning of gondolas*'. No, Rilke had properly felt its rough edges, its latent energies, that spirit '*more potent than the perfume of aromatic lands*', and it irked him that people had so hugely misinterpreted the character of this city.

It was one of the last mornings we would have together. I listened to him, at times distracted by feelings of vague sadness imagining our looming separation. Rilke had expressed the idea of celebrating the happy completion of our work with a special lunch to which he had invited Baladine Klossowska along with my wife. A few days after our last reading hour, I received this note:

Hôtel Foyot, 33, rue de Tournon (VIe).

Dear Friend, I believe I have happened (unless too many errors have crept in) to save you the trouble of returning those two sung verses to be found in the second volume of Malte. *Here is my version.*

It has, it seems to me, the advantage of reproducing little apart from the rhythmic impulse which in the German text makes the voice of the young girl rise above the prose and detach itself from its own development.

This version which was attached to Rilke's letter is here, just as it appeared on the page and just as I transcribed it without modification in the French edition of the *Notebooks*.

> *You, to whom I do not entrust*
> *my long nights without rest,*
> *you who make me so tenderly weary,*
> *rocking me like a cradle;*
> *you who hide from me your sleeplessness,*
> *say, if we could bear*
> *this thirst which magnifies us*
> *without abandonment?*
> *[…]*
> *For remember lovers,*
> *how the lie surprises them*
> *at the hour of confession.*
> *[…]*
> *You alone are part of my pure solitude.*
> *You transform into all: you are this whisper*
> *or this airy scent.*
> *Between my arms: what an abyss that drinks in*
> *losses.*
> *They did not hold you back, and it's thanks to that, surely*
> *that I will never hold you.*
>
> (*Notebooks*, pages 169, 170 and 171)

In this same letter Rilke returned to a detail from another passage we discussed:

> *And for that mark on the floor: if we thought about 'profile', instead of coming up against 'physiognomy'?*

Finally, he proposed a projected lunch date:

As for our lunch engagement: does Tuesday (June 23rd) suit? I would then ask that you and Madame come and collect me from the Foyot, at 12.30pm so that we can either stay there or head off to some other restaurant, depending on how the mood takes us. I clasp your hand affectionately. R.M. Rilke.

During the last visit I received from Rilke we talked once more about Venice and I showed him the little book Lucien Fabre had just published under the title *Bassesse de Venise*,[2] in which he had drawn up a veritable indictment against this city, where 'nothing unforeseen strikes the intelligence', which is only 'false pretense, inhumanity, a call of the innards'.

Although the little I quoted to him seemed to leave Rilke deeply sceptical, he asked me to lend him the work and took it with him that morning.

During the weeks that followed we never had the opportunity to further discuss the charges brought by Lucien Fabre. It was only several months later, after he had left Paris, that the loaned book was returned to me by registered mail. Rilke had attached a cardboard label on which I read:

Madame Klossowska brought back to you the other day certain books you had lent me; so here is another one, which innocently travelled with me: now it comes back to you begging to excuse its escapade. R.

Rilke left the book to speak and himself kept silent. It seemed to him that the accusatory diatribe by Lucien Fabre called for no other response than this silence.

XVII

'FATE HAS THESE HOLES WHERE WE DISAPPEAR'

DURING THE LAST WEEKS of his sojourn in Paris, I only got to see Rilke at longer intervals and rarely alone. It was one day at the publisher of the *Notebooks*, Émile-Paul Frères where we had honoured an appointment along with Edmond Jaloux, then literary director of the house, to sign the contract. On another occasion I accompanied Rilke to a Carnegie Foundation reception.

In the salons of the hotel on boulevard Saint-Germain, he seemed lost and somehow disconsolate. Edmond Jaloux, smiling, already destined for the Académie française, handled with courtesy the assault of professors, ministers and diplomats present. Rilke, surrounded on all sides, searched around for a friendly face, a pretext to evade the prying curiosities. Such exhibitions were onerous for him. However, he had to endure his glory and he was able to present himself with good grace in these moments which caused him fear. A few days later we had lunch in a restaurant in Montmartre with Frédéric Lefèvre, who dedicated one of his interviews in *Les Nouvelles littéraires* to Rilke,[1] and in the crossfire of our questioning Rilke did not come across as too recalcitrant.

Just before that, we had our 'lunch' to celebrate the happy completion of the *Notebooks*. It took place on rue de Valois, on the first floor of Boeuf à la Mode,[2] in a private room decorated with angels of Boucher and unexpected sofas of pink silk. Rilke was plainly happy: he enjoyed choosing the wines himself, relishing a robust Burgundy, celebrating the comparative merits of Spanish and French melons, in good humour right through the meal; he had inaugurated an unknown Rilke, one of the most exuberant cheerfulness. Baladine Klossowska and my wife also attended this lunch, which lingered well into the afternoon. Rilke then took leave of us to pay a visit to his tailor. He might have forgotten this appointment had Baladine Klossowska not reminded him, and which that day meant that he missed the opportunity to take a walk through the Palais Royal.

———

Amongst the French writers to whom I had introduced Rilke was Maurice Martin du Gard,[3] who that year dedicated a portrait to him in *Les Nouvelles littéraires*. This article closed with the following lines: 'There are always the French and there are always the Germans. But there are also poets and this one gave me the taste of fruit that is broken for the first time and whose pure depth is filled with an unknown pleasure.'

Translated in the *Auslandpost*, the article by Martin du Gard was reproduced by a number of German magazines. One of them, *Der Türmer*, seized this opportunity to have a bash at Rilke over his penchant for France:[4]

> It was with a shaking of the head that we read this article devoted to a German poet who once again wanders his vague

reveries through the French capital; and we cannot say that Rilke, who already has an unfortunate bias towards everything that is troubled and confused, has gained anything of note from adopting such an attitude.

In their conversation, reports the French writer, Rilke himself would have said:

Each being in Paris bears a unique expression, a sign of his personality that he does now show, that he does not try to hide either. All the nuances of happiness, of unhappiness, of loneliness, it is on the men of Paris I find them, and French vitality is expressed in the multiplicity of these different appearances; in the street, I never cross a void; I go from one face to the other recalling the sincere and non-approximative value of the first, and everything is immediately filled with a delicate and full light.

It is really difficult for us Germans, whose only concern is to work towards the new greatness of our country, to read such things without a sense of impatience. It is France who makes us suffer most, and here is 'the greatest contemporary lyric poet of Germany' swanning about Paris with his paradoxes, and what's more found 'only there', and not in Germany, upon the faces of men, all the nuances of happiness, unhappiness and solitude. It will be good to remember one day this idiot aesthete's thoughtlessness...

Informed of this attack, Maurice Martin du Gard offered me the columns of his newspaper to fire a riposte to the *Türmer*. But even before I had the leisure to do so a German writer, one Herr Friedrich Märker, had already addressed the pertinent points in a feuilleton from the *Berliner Tagblatt*:

As a German, I feel the need to point out the narrow conception which reveals itself in an article that the *Türmer* published concerning an essay by Maurice Martin du Gard, which appeared in *Les Nouvelles littéraires*, dedicated to Rilke's stay in Paris. The author betrays a state of mind which almost barbarically ignores the role and rights of the poet...

The words 'It will be good to remember one day this idiot aesthete's thoughtlessness' unite as an undisguised threat to the skill of he whom Maurice Martin du Gard had every justification in calling 'the greatest lyric poet of contemporary Germany'. This was an attempt by an independent writer, employing a method more suited to the party political, to distract a public more sheep-like than one endowed with critical acumen. The words 'confused' and 'obscure' will always be the preferred argument in any such campaign. So the fanatics declare themselves 'confused' by anything that falls outside the narrow confines of their programme.

German literature is already so completely monopolized by politics that on the right as on the left it will soon be impossible to find a poet who, in order to earn his crust and get himself into print, will not pursue some political agitation more or less clandestine, or more or less public... Rilke, the poet, like every other man has the right to feel moved by all that is beautiful and exhilarating within or beyond our borders, already diminished enough. Rilke, the poet, has the right to celebrate what he loved in Paris.

And Friedrich Märker concludes:

If I wished to flatter German national pride, I would say: 'Rilke is as enthusiastic about the French as Gauguin was about negroes.'

But since I find that our national pride assumes the appearance of a jealous woman who would demand an overly exclusive adoration from admirers, and would give out the loudest cries at the slightest glance which they would be tempted to bestow upon the beauty of the universe, I say: 'The artist feels most at ease where the human character of things is most apparent.'

Whilst newspapers and reviews fired arguments back and forth over his head, Rilke just wanted to ignore these controversies. He only intervened indirectly to clarify the reasons for his position, when German newspapers in Bohemia insinuated that resentment or annoyance at the miscomprehension of a segment of the German public had orientated him towards France. To Arthur-Fischer Colbrie he wrote:

I would be much pitied if, in my fiftieth year, I admitted in the domain of my art any manifestation of disappointment or bearing a 'grudge', and it is by the most bizarre misunderstandings that this suspicion, so foreign to my nature, was able to project its murky shadow precisely on the production of these French poems which represent for me the most joyful and happy gift, one which is never to expire.

It was summer and Paris was deserted. Once or twice I caught sight of Rilke in the Luxembourg, following an avenue around a block of folded chairs, his step swaying a little. I avoided crossing his path and he did not see me. One evening I learnt that he had just left Paris, abruptly, without farewell, as if suffering from a sudden malaise. It was only in November that I received from him the following letter:

Château de Muzot-sur-Sierre (Valais), Switzerland. This 5th November 1925.

Dear Friend, Unless you have become a collector of rarities, I challenge you to know someone more thankless than me. I am, alas in that regard, perfection—see how long I have gone without writing you a line! That wouldn't excuse me if I let myself confide to you that I have behaved the same towards everyone. Fate sometimes has these holes where we disappear; mine is called discomfort, illness, whatever. I read L'Incertain[5] *(which you had not forgotten to send on to me, inscribing pleasant lines to which I believe, since these favourable feelings towards me, you have practised them more than anyone else... I read your book with attentive interest and hardly tired until the last page. It seems remarkable to me that you even were able to deal with this difficult subject at all, without getting lost in rambling subtleties. We might say that you dominated it by gathering along its thorny hedges an abundant and valuable harvest. All, even that which necessarily obscures it, contributes to making the conflict humanly possible, by preparing, on a higher level, its ever more evident necessity.*

I give you enormous credit for your insistence on bypassing the elusive... the voids that you should have left blank you included as still-vacant land which will be used for future constructions—and you have already established a sort of construction site at the edge of these temporary enclosures.

Also, you were singularly guided to give meaning to such and such internal event; not having neglected any part of this relationship between the visible world and this intrinsic partner who constantly provides the answer, you didn't need to force the drama to which you aspire: it happens, so to speak, on its own. The scene of awakening, so curiously successful (p. 199), seems to me characteristic of certain of your preferred methods.

I found myself, upon receiving your book, prepared for its reading by an article, so fairly judged and insightful, that Emmanuel Bove had dedicated to it in Les Nouvelles littéraires. *His manner of seeing and pronouncing with a plasticity of hesitation is not such a bad thing, it seems to me, with this 'literary criticism' genre that he admits to approaching as an exception and with a certain suspicion. I also understand that he feels more at ease by exercising the surprising faculties of his observation.*

A book, in order to reach us, always wishes to help us; reading does not allow Bove to employ this fruitful restraint which never ceases to establish and inaugurate its unique relationships with reality. It is the 'subject' that must count for him! In Visite d'un soir,[6] *it seems almost replaced by an incessant pleasure of verifying the astonishing change in vital distances. (In my childhood we still subscribed to the custom of 'made-to-measure' gloves; it was quite a peculiar experience offering your hand to the glover. On reading Bove's last book, the memory of this returned to me intact, even down to the physical sensation in my fingers as measurements were taken.)*

Before closing, I must speak to you again about a third book. Whilst drawing it forth the other day, I happened to bring down the colossal pile of mail accumulated here during my interminable absence… the author of this Hélène aux remparts[7] *lives, it would seem, in your house: you must know him. He also spoilt me by writing laudatory words in his volume, which I leafed through with sympathy (why, in passing, had the suspicion dawned on me that this might be a pseudonym, and that Raoul Besançon was inscribed by a feminine nib?).*

It is mobile sentiment, and one that moves without hindrance, that runs through these lines; sometimes he leans on a verse with a certain weariness… in any case, as long as he is known to you, excuse me to this kind author for not having expressed my gratitude as yet…

Rilke had misinterpreted an exact impression: Raoul Besançon was not a woman. But the weariness that Rilke had picked up on in these verses was real enough; however it had other causes.

The letter ended thus:

My solitude, absolute once more and for the whole winter long, brings out clearly in my memory all the opportunities that I did not take full advantage of during my stay in Paris. For example, I would have liked to have seen a great deal more of you. These pages, need I say, are also intended for Madame; it's really the least thing that I can do to occupy the place she wished to reserve for me in her welcoming kindness. And for you, my dear Betz, you well realize, I trust, that beneath the deep layer of my silence still circulates the most friendly concern that I bear towards you and for all time. Kind regards, Rilke.

Arrivals, meetings, departures. Why do these things, when we experience them, remain so veiled to us? When I reread these lines, when I crumple this sheet under my hand, I cannot believe that he could have just left in this way, without me having even suspected that he would never return, and that the long hours that we had spent in each other's company were already, definitively, irremediably the last…

XVIII

MALTE, VERGERS, RECONNAISSANCE À RILKE

LONG MONTHS OF SILENCE separated us, but Rilke knew it was an active silence, where the forms of his mind continued to evolve and through which *The Notebooks of Malte Laurids Brigge* came ever closer to that special life—in short vulgar, and tainted by too many material concerns, that which makes up the printing and publication of a book. This French *Malte* Rilke was now awaiting with some impatience and he revealed this to his Polish translator, Witold Hulewicz,[1] in a letter dated 10th November 1925:

I wish you could delay the definitive printing of the Polish text until the French Malte *appears. This version assumes the full responsibility for my thoughts and, perhaps, owing to the precision and logic of the French language, might aid you in shedding light on certain obscure passages and above all to clarify the relationship between words.*

It is my belief, in fact, that a number of areas which were unclear in the German text will emerge into greater clarity once we view the French. I have such full confidence in this French version, which was in fact due to come out before Christmas...

However, it was not until the spring of 1926 that a letter brought Rilke the news that the proofs of his book were being corrected, and at the same time posed numerous questions to him relating to the project, to which we had conspired to dedicate an entire issue of the *Cahiers du mois*. He replied to me on 26th April, and although dated from the Val-Mont sanatorium, this letter, which was very detailed, did not neglect to give me any of the information I had asked him for.

Val-Mont, by Glion-sur-Territet (Vaud), Switzerland. This 26th April 1926.

Dear Friend, this silence of which you make honourable amends is, in short, only half mine and our common regrets unite us, having reciprocal value; I knew you took good care of me, and my plenipotentiary to you, Malte, had not been recalled by any silence.

I am so pleased to learn that you are content now that your long labours are at an end. We can honestly say to ourselves, both of us, that we have omitted nothing which would not lead to a positive outcome for this translation; this effort has already given us certain reward 'avant la lettre': *that, amongst others, of having been able to spend these delectable hours filled with that laborious concordance which you kindly give mention and of which I too guard the most intimate memory.*

Edmond Jaloux, whom I met in Lausanne ten days ago and whom I hope to see again soon, also talked about these upcoming publications, intended to see the light of day simultaneously (for the selection of my poems written in French, Vergers,[2] *will also be released in all likelihood in May).*

As for this cahier amongst the Cahiers du mois *that you had thought of dedicating to me, I have been a little fearful that the natural dearth of material may cause you some troubled thoughts. And I am not sure how to make up for it. My German publisher Insel, I hope, at my instigation, will have lent you some critical texts relating to my work. I was informed that the book by M.R.H. Heygrodt*[3] *(which I believe will be amongst these printed papers) contains some instructive insights (you'll recall I have little knowledge of all this secondary literature and I only wish to maintain my innocence in that regard...). However, I will have a friend from Zurich forward to you two more recent works which I request that you return to him after you have finished with them.*

And here are the addresses you were asking for: It's Mme Inga Junghanns, in Copenhagen K..., who achieved a really beautiful translation of Malte, *following on from the Rodin book and the* Cornet. *As for my translator in Poland, it would be M. Witold Hulewicz, Wilno... For the translations formerly produced in Russia, it is I think M. Michel Zetlin who could provide you with some details; he himself had taken great care to render versions of selected poems, and he has always shown a most friendly deference towards me. M. Zetlin resides in Paris.*

If by chance M. Johan Bojer, the Norwegian novelist, well known in France, happened to be presently in Paris, I feel sure he would agree to offer you a few lines on my writings and our old rapport. A portion of my work, somewhat restricted I think, was translated in Holland, England, Italy and Spain; but of these versions I have no knowledge at all; I am not even privy to the names of the translators.

Le Convegno *(a leading art review in Milan) had published in one of its most recent issues some of my older poems, excellently translated by one M. Gianturco; another Italian journal has just announced further translations due to the attention of Madame la Princesse von Thurn und Taxis. The* Rodin, *a selection of poems and a third volume were, quite some time ago now, published in America; but again, on this subject I have no further details.*

What a shame that the great Verhaeren is no longer here to recount to you the fervent confidence which he placed in me, and which for long years I could draw on for the greatest comfort. I told you something about him and

I hesitate to tell you more, so as not to cover up by the weight of the written word the accents of my voice, so what you already have can be protected.

What particularly saddens me is not having anything very personal to offer you for this friendly 'cahier'. Impossible from here to sift through my old papers in Muzot, and as for any new papers, Val-Mont was hardly the place to fill a page with writing. I reveal to you my dearth, dear friend: nothing! This note from the Urgeräusch *(the title is not mine) would be too little. Wouldn't you find more in the issue that the Prager Presse dedicated to me? The writer of this literary supplement surprised me by having unearthed (from God knows where) these fragments of the* Traumbuch *that I had completely forgotten (the whole book was never done).*[4] *Cast an eye over this prose and the issue as a whole, the content of which must have been composed by someone who has done a fine job of leafing through my texts.*

You speak to me of Mme X... No! She can't offer anything but a few dedications of a personal nature which lack any literary interest. I will always refuse these 'second-hand items' which lose all their value when taking leave of the person who owns them. I would be the first to accept the collaboration of a happy coincidence; but in this case, we should let it lie.

Leafing through my pocket notebooks (both of which accompanied me here), I find nothing there either save for a scattering of verses, still in French (because I continue, I must confess, to cultivate this little violin by Ingres, made from the wood of a dubious cherry tree). Should I resist the temptation to copy out for you a few samples?

In matters of art indulgence should remain firmly out of the picture. I therefore cannot even invoke yours. You will have to see if you can find something amongst these lines worthy of representing me in the Cahiers du mois. *If you wish to have me whole, you must not conceal my fundamental weaknesses.*

Excuse the somewhat improvised and hasty nature of these lines; we don't write quite as we would like here and I especially wanted not to keep you hanging on. My recollections to Madame, my very best to her and to you, dear friend, my full and friendly gratitude. R.M. Rilke.

Several PSs completed this long message:

I hope that the concern over our Malte *has not caused too much of an interruption to your own production? I was under the impression a new work had been announced, or at least promised?*

If the little notebook of my few copied verses (a very poor notebook as one finds here), gives you pleasure, please hang on to it. It goes without saying that these essays, dating from a later time, do not appear in Vergers.

It is also difficult for me to decide here on those copies of the French Malte *which I would like to send. I don't have all the addresses to hand that I would need to give you. It would for this reason be preferable that I bring in the finished volumes later on, to send them out myself. By that time I hope to have returned to my Muzot, abandoned since 20th December!*

My mailouts to friends of my Valéry translations were interrupted by my departure for Val-Mont, I had very recently brought here the copy which was intended for you: it will follow in a few days. Please remember me to Emmanuel Bove; I try my utmost to follow him, and I read, with the same level of attention I apply to all his writings, that curious and intense short story published in Œuvres libres[5] *R.*

But the final page proofs of *The Notebooks of Malte Laurids Brigge* were completed. Already a few articles had been collected in a file by the editorial staff of the *Cahiers du mois* on which are traced these words: *Reconnaissance à Rilke.*[6]

Daniel Rops, Jean Cassou, Marcel Brion were amongst the first to respond to our call. Others soon joined them: Edmond

Jaloux, Francis de Miomandre, Geneviève Bianquis, Félix Bertaux, Franz Hellens, Jacques Benoist-Méchin, André Germain, André Berge... all provisional testimonies whose deficiency we sense. So as an epigraph to our *Cahier* we wrote this sentence by Rilke:

For fame is ultimately only the sum of the misunderstandings that gather around a new name.

But this book is meant to be a rallying call, a starting point. 'This Tribute', I wrote, by way of warning, 'will only garner its full force if we are willing to perceive, under the conscious and motivated cohesion that we find there, the echo of a more secret vibration, and between the distinct voices of those who already speak there, the obscure and distant chorus of all the more intimate testimonies which have not yet come through to us.'

Valéry was one of the first readers of *Vergers*, Rilke's French poems, which was to appear at the instigation of the *Nouvelle Revue française*. Rilke had translated it—in such an impressive manner, it would be worth showing it in detail!—'and with so much respect and joyfulness', as he put it to Pierre Klossowski, both *Charmes* and *Eupalinos*.[7] In our view there was really no way Valéry could be absent from our tribute. One morning, François Berge and I set off to rue de Villejust to fill him in on our project. 'Just give us a page or two, that's all we ask,' we beseeched him. 'Two pages? But that would mean eight days of work!' exclaimed Valéry, whilst at the same time assuring us that he was naturally keen to express the gratitude and affection he felt for Rilke. Valéry rather exaggerated his slowness, as just three days later I received the piece which has so often been quoted since then and where the figure of Rilke stands out in decorative relief upon the ancient walls of Muzot:

Rilke, my dear Rilke, to whom my verses owe their resounding in a language of which I know nothing—everything conspires to take away my leisure and almost my power to state in clear terms what I feel about you. I would like to leave here a certain grace that can only come from calmness and time. Such rich possessions are withheld from me. Too many myriad demons compete for the substance of my hours.

Do you remember how surprised I was by that extreme solitude in which I found you when I first met you? I was passing by; you caused me to halt en route to Italy, and took me in for a spell. A very small castle tower terribly alone on a vast site below rather mournful mountains; antique and pensive rooms, with dark furniture, closed-in days, all of this gripped my heart. My imagination could not help but listen in to your infinite interior monologue of a completely isolated consciousness, which nothing can distract from itself and that feeling of being unique.

I could not imagine such a separate existence, eternal winters in such an excess of intimacy with silence, so much unlimited freedom offered to your dreams, to those essential and overly concentrated spirits which we find in the books, to the inconstant geniuses of writing, to the powers of memory.

Dear Rilke, who to me seemed sealed off in pure time, I feared for you in this transparency of a too even-tempered life which, over unchanging days, allows death to be clearly seen.

How easy it was for me to lament for you, whilst your thoughts created marvels out of this void, and made mother the longevity! Enviable amongst all others is your home, the low tower, the enchanted tower of Muzot. This frightening peace, this greatness of tranquillity now appears to me what they always were for you, the most delicious conditions.

If by magic they were bestowed on me, I could probably accomplish the sweet labour of painting in words the admirable form of your soul. I don't know even one of these most famous and beautiful works. My ignorance forbids me. But I know it from a more direct intuition, I divine what it expects, I perceive the depth, I sense its infinite resonance; and nothing is more precious to me than its gentle friendship, all imbued with that mysterious sensibility which lies within you.

Some foreign testimonies completed our tribute to Rilke, which was to reveal, by a surprising unanimity of judgement, what a central position this solitary actually occupied in European literature. An evasive Thomas Mann claimed too heavy a workload and generously reminded us of the refusals he had already made to similar requests from German journals. Rudolf Kassner, who was travelling, was never to receive my letter. He later wrote to me: 'Too bad I'm not exactly adept at such tributes, but for my friend Rilke I would have been more than happy to give it my best shot.'

On the other hand, the Spaniards Antonio Marichalar and José Bergamín, whom we managed to reach through the diligence of Jean Cassou, evoked the passage of Rilke, 'that grey pilgrim concentrated in himself', through a Spain where he had gone to absorb the light. Christian Rimestad recalled the figures of Jacobsen and Obstfelder and Rilke's relationship to Denmark. Many other voices answered our call: Mme Hélène von Nostitz and Paul Zech for Germany, H. Marsmann for Holland, Tivadar Raith for Hungary, Nino Frank for Italy, Witold Hulewicz for Poland, Max Rychner for Switzerland, Camill Hoffmann for Czechoslovakia...

The little *carnet de poche* of verses that Rilke had confided to me found its place in our book almost in its entirety, and I sent the proofs to Rilke himself. I was never so keen on those responses when his politeness takes on too humble a form.

Val-Mont, by Glion-sur-Territet (vaud), Switzerland. This 28th May 1926.

Dear Friend, on this occasion, for reasons of speed, I must resign myself to being brief, although your penultimate letter left me with the need to tell you many a word of spontaneous and emotional gratitude. I barely wanted to be able to believe that you could judge worthy of inclusion in the Cahiers du mois *this entire suite detached from a 'carnet de poche'.*

Isn't this showing a little too much condescension to this production of my second lyre?... I don't dare, however, to oppose any decisions you have made, and here are the proofs, where I found only a few corrections to make. I attach some genealogical remarks, and I accompany the whole with my most amicable sympathy, shaking your hand affectionately. R.M. Rilke

The genealogical notes to which Rilke alludes were to complete the biographical notice intended for our *Cahier*. They are as follows:

Coat of arms: between sable and silver, two greyhounds rampant, opposite another (without bequeath).

According to ancient tradition, my family is connected (having always borne these same arms) to the Rilkes of Carinthia that we find mentioned there amongst the nobility, dating from 1276; a separate branch settled in Saxony at the end of the fifteenth century. From there at different times, many family members emigrated to Bohemia, where my great-grandfather owned the castle of Kamenice n. L.

Rilke attached great importance to these questions, which on occasion caused irritation to some of his friends.

'Deep down, there was a snob in him, worse, an adventurer,' declared Mme Lou Albert-Lasard one day. 'I actually said as much to his face, in a moment of temper. His blue blood, his noble origin, it was all just make believe. The truth of it was that his family came from half-Saxon, half-Carinthian peasant stock and his grandfather was a steward!'

Les Cahiers de Malte Laurids Brigge finally appeared in July 1926, almost at the same moment as *Vergers* and *Reconnaissance à Rilke*. The poet anticipated these books with more impatience than we had supposed. An inattention on behalf of the publisher almost clouded his joy. Barely had the first copies been dispatched to Val-Mont, where we imagined he still was, than I received telegram from Muzot which read:

Sierre 2. 40. 10.45. And our Notebooks, *dear friend, which, it seems, have arrived? I have not yet seen the shadow of a copy. Remind me with my compliments to our editors.—Rilke.*

I hastened to send Rilke the only copy I had on hand, explaining to him the delay that had occurred. He replied to me on 3rd July:

Dear Friend, in fact, I should have immediately let you know of my return to Muzot; I do not believe, however, that a package addressed to Val-Mont could have gone astray, since a large part of my mail comes to me via this detour.

> *Now, holding in my hands, truly existing and perfectly real, this first copy that you have so promptly addressed to me, I have all the patience required to await further copies the publisher is preparing for me. These copies will be ten in number, according to what you tell me; as soon as I receive them, I can then ascertain how many more I shall require, and I will let you know, if you'll permit me.*
>
> *Right now, I am fully occupied with sending out* Vergers. *May this little book remind you of your old plans to pass by the Valais and commit yourself to an upcoming fulfilment. What a shame that we can't have dinner tonight, with a place laid for Malte as well. Madame would too, I feel, wear a radiant complexion beside this neighbour she frequented so much in your company.*
>
> *Be assured, dear and active friend, of my affection, your R.M. Rilke.*

A few days later, another letter, the last of this summer: Rilke complains that the volumes he has received are marked 'fourth edition' and asks me to pass on his disapproval to the publisher. A quick message, written at speed, for Rilke is about to depart for Ragaz, where he will meet up with Princess von Thurn und Taxis:

> *... I am leaving for Ragaz any day, which means I am writing to you rather hastily. Do you have any agreeable plans for the holidays and are you going to take them soon? All my best wishes for a bountiful summer on your part, consenting for your need for repose and calm or to complete some cherished work!*

An additional shipment of volumes of the *Notebooks* was made by Émile-Paul, who responded directly to Rilke. How many further volumes, though, were already on their way, heading—by what detours?—towards the hearts that awaited them...

XIX

THE LAST SUMMER OF RAINER MARIA RILKE

WHAT THIS LAST SUMMER was like for Rilke, I only know through indirect testimonies.

In August he left for Ragaz, as his letter announced. For the third time he was to meet Princess von Thurn und Taxis, but his state of health obliged him to cut short his stay in the autumn. But on the upside, when taking the waters at this old Swiss bathing resort which he really adored, he met a Belgian family, and in particular a child, a girl of thirteen, whose perfection enchanted him.

'He talked to me about her,' said Edmond Jaloux, who saw him again the following month in Lausanne, 'declaring her one of the most accomplished beings he had ever encountered on this earth. Beauty, experience, maturity and the gift of poetry inhabiting this child had left an indelible memory on his mind. He spoke shakily of her future, horror-struck to imagine what damage loathsome daily reality could wreak on this being of such rare purity.'

September saw him again on the shore of Lake Geneva, savouring those last diaphanous days of summer of a rare serenity. André Germain encountered him in Lausanne, at the Hôtel

Savoy, seeking animation and a friendly face before retreating to his stone trunk of Muzot. Willingly the poet lingers in the hotel lobby, where he meets up with Edmond Jaloux and his wife.

'Won over again to the socialite life', he delights in 'the elegant make-up of this palace, with its too-convenient brightness, with its women and its flowers, and especially at the sight he loves, the view opening on to a landscape as smiling as it is noble, grey mountains which descend like a line of verse, smoothly, learnedly, to lose themselves in the blue of the lake.'

A surprising encounter marks the close of this summer: a meeting with 'a woman who was stepping out', as André Germain informs us, 'as if from a fairy tale, and who, upright, slender, dazzling, carried him away with the fullness of her gestures and the variety of her expressions, the glamour and flattery of the East and that winning smile which, for us, is forever affixed to the prow of a boat powerfully carving the subjugated waters of Cydnus...'[1]

He also sees Paul Valéry again, passing through Geneva, whom he then joins in Anthy near Thonon-les-Bains to talk over his translation of *Narcisse*.[2] Whilst strolling beneath the lofty trees of the Parc d'Anthy, the two poets discuss the specific meaning that Valéry lent this myth. Embracing his friend, Rilke questions him: 'I was speaking', says Valéry,

> and he was taking part in my words, in my enterprise, in order to make exist for him alone that which did not yet exist and will perhaps never exist; he took part as a poet takes part in himself, like one who stands at the interior, which is itself assailed on all sides by ideas, seductions, impediments, illuminations, inclinations, resolutions and renouncements, by all that constitutes the interior life of a poem.

Then Rilke embarks on the little white paddle steamer which was to take him back to Lausanne. The two poets part company. 'And there was nothing left but a trace of foam and a smoke which vanished.'

———

In October Rilke returned to Muzot. Towards the end of the month he received a little novel that I had started the previous winter, during a stay in Provence, and that the recent summer had allowed me to complete. It is of this book that Rilke, already in the grip of illness, speaks to me in the last letter I received from him:

Château de Muzot-sur-Sierre (Valais) Switzerland. This 29th October 1926.

My dear friend, I have just got over a bad intestinal flu which, after several days of fever, left me in a state of almost anonymous weakness: see only in the lines which follow my desire to be amongst the first to congratulate you on Le Démon impur.[3]

I received your book yesterday; I have read it twice since, the second time out loud, and I am now setting out on my third reading. The first was all astonishment, the second, I have no hesitation in telling you, was merely a constantly admiring application… the third I anticipate will demonstrate to me the possibility of conjoining these two spontaneous reactions to form for you within me a singular and intimate glory.

My dear Betz, I don't know how you pulled it off, but with this powerful book, so well constructed and which contains no emptiness, no vagueness, no provisory subterfuge, you have gone straight from apprenticeship into the ranks of those who are the representatives of the noble métier and who, from now on, see themselves permitted to employ their intrinsic freedom in the highest and most definitive obedience.

From start to finish, this book seems to me to have obeyed the most secret necessity of its subject. No secondary attempt could distract you from it; once the slope is established the river of action flows down it according to the law of the waters. The consequences, prepared from afar, appear at the right moment, nothing orchestrated, nothing forced, nothing intentional. A change of climate around a landscape of soul, and here is a whole new vital vegetation that you knew how to let take root by enclosing it with the universal rhythm which understands the absurd, as it understands the ambition, which does not know...

I would only be at the beginning if I were to list all the reasons for my support; for me there are several occurring on every page. I really admired the precision of your images, this detached and infinitely malleable style that you have developed, unless you just found everything in place when the time came... Freed from those interior analogies which were both the charm and the peril of your first books, you found at your disposal not only a considerable sum of observations, but full power to proceed as an imperturbable and shrewd observer.

What a tremendous discovery! It has overtaken, it seems to me, the construction site and it is, dear friend, to your life in its entirety that I send my congratulations: only a surging up of all-embracing life force was able to permit you the perfect, pure success of such a book!

I cannot close these lines without indicating my confusion for not having thanked anyone yet (not even you, nor your friends, Messrs Berge), of this rare testimony represented by Reconnaissance à Rilke. *Over the last months I have read this or that page at random. I am fearful of the power of these mirrors, and passing from one to the other I hide from my own image. How much ignorance of what I have achieved is natural and dear to me! I am ashamed of holding on to it all so much, but I foresee that I will never possess the courageous curiosity to compare myself to all these testimonies, so unique in their tact and generosity.*

> *Which, moreover, hardly prevents me from feeling a deep gratitude towards the very act of this 'cahier' about which I hope to speak of to others as I go along, as my strength permits.*
>
> *Is it true that you were in Constantinople?*
>
> *Please, my dear Betz, remember me to Madame and find here the warmth of my two hands and that of my enthusiasm, which you knew how to rouse. My very best to you, Rilke.*
>
> *P.S. Did Emmanuel Bove know your book before it was published? He must I feel sure be very keen on it. But to how many of our friends* Le Démon impur *would have been a surprise, a revelation as it will surely be for the majority of literary critics.*

Rilke was sadly mistaken: *Le Démon impur* scarcely attracted any literary criticism and his approval was my surest respondent. I would even have been tempted to believe that our friendship had influenced his praise if I had not known since that, in a letter addressed around the same time to a friend in Zurich, Mme Wunderly-Volkart,[4] he urged her to read the book and expressed his enthusiasm in clear terms: '*That book was a real event for me… an almost magisterial assurance… I was overcome with admiration.*'

To show gratitude for such a gift, how much, alas, clumsiness and artifice are that much more easily accessible to us than the unadorned truth.

The letter I wrote to Rilke that day I found, after his death, unfinished. Annoyed with myself, I had abandoned it on the table, then buried it in a drawer. Did I sense that the reflection of my preoccupations in that moment was simply not worthy to appear before his face, already masked by a deathly shadow? The truth is that I had simply not suspected an outcome so severe. We still hoped for his return, we expected it.

Before heading to Toulon, where he thought more and more about settling down, we assumed that he would return to Paris, where his friends were all asking for him and where he even had a rendezvous planned with Princess von Thurn und Taxis.

In December, assembled at the home of Baladine Klossowska, with André Gide, Edmond Jaloux, Charles Du Bos, Pierre Jean Jouve, Marc Allégret and a few others, we passed from hand to hand a telegram announcing his arrival in Val-Mont which contained words of optimism. Suddenly, during the last days of December, in the midst of the holidays, late in the afternoon, a message, a disturbing presence, I didn't know from where, came...

I just couldn't take it in; I still refused to accept it as I climbed the narrow staircase that led to Klossowska's studio.

I knock, the door opens. '*How is Rilke?*' He was dead.

RILKE ALIVE

FRIENDS DISCUSS A DEATH. Bitter consolation over the details: he refused injections, he desired his own death, before leaving Muzot he had put all his papers in order, rolled up his carpets, marked each object, as if departing on a great journey.

We accompanied him to the cemetery of Raron. Someone chose a headstone, planted a rose bush, had a verse engraved there. Then the months pass. A drawing of him, a letter reread… exchanges of memories, late regrets. The missed opportunities that cannot come again. That neglected question, that too-weak response, that visit to Isabelle Rivière, to talk about Alain-Fournier, but she did not know his name and found out too late who he was. And still the months pass. The wind leafs through the open books which we have left aside until spring. Can mourning really so quickly become a habit?

In the first days of fine weather, when the little children's carrousel of the Luxembourg begins to turn, I know that I could make him out at a distance, there amongst the trees. The magnolias, will they blossom soon? Are the roses already set for summer?

But he still moves close to me in many other ways. Unannounced visits: mostly women, many women… they opine on him, they clutch like a missal some touching image of a time so distant that their dreams seem to have been preserved there as if only by some miracle.

Of him they know little or nothing, since they easily fall back into the resentments that followed the departure, or in the memoirs that expose them. For themselves they guard the purest, that most secret sanctuary.

Some owe him almost everything. He showed them the reflection that he saw of them, and since that moment they have applied themselves to upholding it more and more. So soon we will no longer know which was true: the woman or the image.

Others have already forgotten. They offer letters when it is a question of the anemones of Muzot, the gardens of Paris, winters in Sweden or the sun of Provence. One hundred francs for a meeting, two hundred for a three-page letter. Were these the ones Rilke took pity on when he met them, sitting in some cold museum hall, before an easel, or on the staircase of a Parisian hotel? Would he think that they only deny him to free themselves from the heavy burden of a memory?

And the letters, so many letters! Rilke received immeasurable quantities. Customarily he responded to them:

There are so many people who expect something from me, I don't know quite what—help, counsel... The experiences of Malte sometimes force me to respond to these cries issued by strangers, for he would have done so, he left me with a legacy of action, in that I should not turn back from a charitable destination.

Only then do we begin to get the full measure of what comes from afar and travels far, this wave of which we saw only a crest of foam.

There is the legionnaire, lost somewhere in deepest Africa, who read *The Book of Hours* and employs his moments of rest to translate the poems.

There is the Brazilian woman who had not yet received the news of Rilke's death and would very much like to talk to him about Rodin, whom she once knew.

There is the friend of the poet who sent me the 'words of his heart'. Namely a photograph of Raron, sent by an unknown hand.

There is the student who has read the *Notebooks* and who waits impatiently for the *Letters to a Young Poet*.[1]

There is the distant reader who writes to me from the depths of her valley in the Cantal:

> Would Rilke—I am so envious that you knew him personally—be happy to know his thoughts live in a peaceful house bordering a stream? Would he be happy to know that with one of his books between her fingers a young woman often falls silent?

―――

And then, one evening, there stands in front of me, in the same room where I worked with Rilke, this young Dane, fresh, vital, flanked by a huge, sporty-looking, broad-shouldered Norwegian with powerful hands. This was Inga Junghanns, who sang Bellmann's lieder for Rilke when he was in Munich, and who later felt drawn to translate the *Notebooks* into Danish.[2] She had written to Rilke in 1923:

> If you go to Paris next May, I will let Gide know and I would like to recommend a young poet there (around twenty-four years of age), who is already in the process of translating *Malte*.

The young poet was me. I was about the age that Rilke attributed to me then, but he never mentioned to me anything about Inga Junghanns; I only knew of her existence two years after his death when she paid me that visit.

It is without sadness that we speak of him, rather with laughter and raised voices that remind me of the Schulin family who feature in the *Notebooks*. Inga tells me of her first meeting with Rilke, in Munich—where, ignoring his great work and renown, she sang to him for hours, without the least timidity, those tunes of Bellmann he loved so much—then the visit that she received from him in 1919, in a village in the Engadin.

We can well imagine them, gathered round a table in a small, low kitchen, an intimate and cheerful Danish atmosphere, whilst the madeira pancakes crackle in the frying pan on the stove. Inga Junghanns, her husband and their friend, all laughing, all joyous, like a child on his birthday.

They talk about Copenhagen, tell stories of the Friesian fishermen, they nibble olives which remind them of Rilke's Paris and Provence, they pass without transition from one serious conversation to outpourings of unbridled laughter for no real reason.

Rilke stayed with Inga Junghanns three days longer than he had originally intended, then he took the diligence to return to Soglio.

It was again Inga Junghanns that he approached when, a few months later, in this half-Italian town, he wanted to decorate a Christmas tree. Indeed, who better than this Danish friend could have chosen the candles of different colours, the little Jesus Christ and the nuts of gold for this celebration of exile whose date, since then, has been confused with the anniversary of his death?

But, he wrote to Regina Ullmann,

birthdays have no true importance; our birthdays are birthdays without a spiritual number and have little to do with what the heart can contribute to the world.

———

A few days ago, when I was writing these lines, a letter from Switzerland informed me that Rilke's grave was in a sorry state of neglect.

Autumn, the sodden earth, the last rusting foliage, the feet sinking into the mud, the cold wind bending the poplars, fatal images of this late season of death! But we can stay true to a memory without concerning ourselves with the inclement weather to which it remains exposed.

The rose bush that friendly hands planted on the tomb at Raron will know to flower without any human's help.

For me, who failed to visit Muzot when invited so often by Rilke, there is a genuine sense of anticipation in seeing the tomb at Raron. And if, someday soon, I have the urge to meet up with him, I know another place, more secret, where one can find his company.

In one of the countless rooms of the Louvre, somewhere, beneath a window, in the recess, is a small Venetian mirror, framed by onyx columns inlaid with emeralds, medallions and old amber.

I know that one day Rilke looked at this mirror, which once belonged to Marie de Médicis. Amidst so many faces whose reflection has worn away its unsettled tint, which goes on mirroring the whiteness of the Parisian sky in its prison of glass, I know his face was contained there.

Mirrors, even now have we ever learnedly spoken
of what in essence you are?
Intervals of time,
empty spaces, like sieves…
Some seem to have passed into you,
others, you let them go, mistrustful…

Was it then retained or allowed to escape, this face which one day drew close to the cold surface, doubtless with more warmth, more tender intelligence than so many others?

Between the sarcophagi of the pharaohs, the ruins of Assyrian temples, paintings by Rubens or Leonardo and the jewels of the Galerie d'Apollon, this intact mirror preserves in its passage through time something more certain and true than all the testimonies forged by pen or chisel: the image we place there because we carry it within us.

OCTOBER–NOVEMBER 1936

Maurice Betz—A Poet and Literary Translator in Paris

Maurice Betz was not just the pioneering translator of Rilke into the French language, but an accomplished poet and novelist in his own right, a view which was consolidated for Rilke as he read more works by Betz and was initially largely the reason why he felt this *Alsacien* would be the ideal translator of his own poetry and prose into French. Rilke also had a certain nostalgia for the region, as he had published his first book in Strasbourg in 1897. Betz had completed his secondary education in Colmar and continued to promote the creative riches of the region until the end of his life. Betz discovered the poetry of Rilke at age seventeen during a period of study at the Faculté des Lettres in Neuchâtel, as articulated so vividly in the text of *Conversations with Rilke*. He then joined the Foreign Legion, taking Rilke with him. After the armistice in 1918 he settled in Paris, in rooms at 1, rue de Médicis which would remain his Parisian address and where seven years later he would receive Rilke. He enjoyed a vigorous literary lifestyle in Paris, regularly attending ballet, concerts and opera, and began to publish under a pseudonym, Maurice Devire, most notably an anthology on his native Alsace. He then embarked on a period of study of law at the Sorbonne, becoming a lawyer at the Cour de Paris.

In 1921 he published his first collection of poems, *Scaferlati for the Troops*, before publishing the crucial fragment from *The Notebooks of Malte Laurids Brigge* in *Les Contemporains*. Betz directed the *Cahiers du mois* from 1924 to 1928, producing a series of novels at the same time reputedly influenced by Gide and Dostoyevsky. With the success of the translation of Rilke's *Notebooks*, the young translator, flushed with praise from the likes of Gide, Valéry and Jaloux, became an editorial advisor to publisher Émile-Paul Frères at 14, rue de l'Abbaye and exclusive translator of Rilke's works. Betz proceeded with this prestigious task at a feverish pace and alongside Rilke managed to fit in translations of Thomas Mann, Ernst Jünger, Goethe and Nietzsche. The diverse selection from Rilke's oeuvre included *Histoires du bon Dieu* in 1927, the monograph *Rodin* in 1928, *Fragments en prose* in 1929, *Contes de Bohême* in 1939 and *Journal florentin* in 1946. Still more Rilke translations were published with other presses, such as *Petite Stèle pour Rainer Maria Rilke* with J. Heissler in 1927 (including fifteen poems from *The Sonnets to Orpheus*), *Le Livre des rêves* with J. Schiffrin in 1928 and *Lettres sur Cézanne* with Corrêa in 1944.

Following his *Rilke vivant* in 1937, Betz turned his attention to Germany, of which he was something of a connoisseur, publishing *Portrait de l'Allemagne* in 1939, the year war broke out. He followed this with the valuable collection *Dialogues des prisonniers* in 1941, sourced from his brief period of soldierly captivity in France after the defeat in 1940. Following his release Betz worked as an interpreter for a time and mediator with the German authorities for French prisoners of war, whilst forging on with his Rilke translations for Émile-Paul Frères. Incredibly, Betz managed one Rilke publication per year even during the darkest years of occupation: *Le Chant de l'amour et de la mort du Cornette Christoph Rilke* in 1940, *Le Poète* in 1941 and *Le Paysage* in 1942. By now Betz had to all intents and purposes taken on the role of Rilke's literary executor in France. At the end of the war he assembled *Alsace perdue et retrouvée*, an anthology of writers celebrating his home region. This appeared in 1946, just before Maurice Betz died unexpectedly aged only forty-seven on 31 October 1946, alone in a hotel room in Tours, far from his wife and home.

Betz left behind a number of literary projects in various stages of completion. One of these was his half-finished translation of letters between Rilke and Magda von Hattingberg, alias 'Benvenuta'. This was finished by another hand and published posthumously in 1947. Further projects on the Betz desk, albeit in embryonic form, had been Rilke's letters to Baladine Klossowska, alias 'Merline', and those to Hélène von Nostitz, whom he had personally met in Paris in 1943. His novel *Souvenirs du bonheur* was published through the efforts of his widow posthumously in 1949. In the same year an *Hommage à Maurice Betz* appeared in honour of the writer who had been admired and loved by his peers. This contained often moving tributes from a wide range of writers and academics from Germany, France, Austria and Switzerland, who had known Betz in Paris or elsewhere during the inter-war years. The *Hommage*, published by who else but Émile-Paul Frères, also included letters by Rilke and Betz himself, as well as excerpts from Betz's journals and notebooks, hitherto unpublished. In 1957 a literary prize, the 'Prix Maurice Betz', was set up in Alsace by Mme Betz in memory of her husband.

SELECTED TRANSLATIONS BY MAURICE BETZ

Vicki Baum, *Lohwinckel en folie*, Émile-Paul Frères, 1932
— *Le Dernier Jour*, Émile-Paul Frères, 1938
— *Sang et volupté à Bali*, Stock, 1939
Goethe, *Élégies romaines*, Émile-Paul Frères, 1944
Ernst Jünger, *Jardins et routes*, Plon, 1942
Thomas Mann, *La Montagne magique*, Fayard, 1931
Friedrich Nietzsche, *Ainsi parlait Zarathoustra*, Gallimard, 1936

Rainer Maria Rilke, *Les Cahiers de Malte Laurids Brigge*, Émile-Paul Frères, 1925
— *Histoires du bon Dieu*, Émile-Paul Frères, 1927
— *Le Livre des rêves*, J. Schiffrin, 1928
— *Poésie*, Émile-Paul Frères, 1938
— *Chant de l'amour et de la mort du Cornette Christoph Rilke*, Émile-Paul Frères, 1940
— *Lettres sur Cézanne*, Corrêa, 1944
— *Fragments sur la guerre*, Émile-Paul Frères, 1944-45
— *Journal florentin*, Émile-Paul Frères, 1946
— *Rilke et Benvenuta. Lettres et souvenirs*, Denoël, 1947
Carl Sternheim, *Napoléon et autres récits*, Presses universitaires, 1924
Marie von Thurn und Taxis, *Souvenirs sur Rainer Maria Rilke*, Émile-Paul Frères, 1936

Translator's Acknowledgements

I must here humbly issue thanks to my publisher Pushkin Press for their patience and faith in the final manifestation of this translation. For their valuable contribution to matters concerning the text, I am grateful to artist and illustrator Bridget Strevens and freelance editor Linden Lawson. The totality of my remaining gratitude must necessarily be channelled to one person, the American poet and editor Katie Lehman, who nobly assisted with the hard labour of compiling the Notes and protracted general fettling of the manuscript. The impact of her selfless support cannot be overstated.

Notes

ON THE DISCOVERY OF RILKE

1 St Peter's Island is situated in Lake Biel at the foot of the Jura Mountains in western Switzerland. The island-turned-peninsula measures 5km in length and just less than 1km at its widest point. Jean-Jacques Rousseau sought refuge here in 1765, finding a place of rare peace and serenity. Today pilgrims still arrive by boat across the lake to enjoy the scenery and follow the winding path Rousseau took around the island.

2 Marcel Hofer (1896–1978) was a French-speaking Swiss writer who bore the pseudonym of Lucien Marsaux. Hofer began his career in law but switched to literature, leaving behind a large body of work of some twenty-five volumes. Those mentioned by Betz are *Le Carnaval des vendanges* and *Les Prodigues*, published by Plon in 1929 and 1930 respectively.

3 The edition *Bibliotheca Romanica* or *Bibliothèque française* was published in Strasbourg and edited by J.H. Heitz. The series included classic French texts and was distributed throughout Europe and as far as New York.

4 The *Mercure de France* originated as a literary magazine in the seventeenth century and, following various metamorphoses, experienced a renaissance in the 1890s when it took to publishing books alongside the review. Since 1995, it has been part of the Gallimard group.

5 Commonly known as the *NRF*, *La Nouvelle Revue française* is a prominent literary magazine in France dating from 1909. The *NRF*'s aim was to remain impartial and beyond any faction or creed. Between the world wars, under the legendary editorships of Jacques Rivière and Jean Paulhan, it established itself as the country's leading literary journal. In 1940, under a new editor, it took a pro-fascist line and ceased publication in 1943. After due sentence for collaboration it was revived in 1953, with Paulhan back at the helm, and eventually became a quarterly. Today the editor is Antoine Gallimard, whose famous publishing house was originally an offshoot of the magazine.

6 *Die Weise von Liebe und Tod des Cornets Christoph Rilke* is a poem in prose which Rilke wrote apparently over a single night in 1899 and published in 1906. When it was revised and republished in 1912 it was a runaway success, selling out almost immediately and bringing Rilke's name to the

fore. This tale of a soldier from the Austro-Turkish wars of the 1660s struck a chord with modern soldiers and many would include a copy in their packs when they were drawn into a European war a few years later. The first French edition was duly translated by Betz and published by Émile-Paul Frères in 1940.

7   J.-H. Rosny aîné was a pseudonym for Joseph Henri Honoré Boex (1856–1940), a Brussels-born author who wrote in French. After 1909 Joseph Henri began using 'senior' ('*aîné*') after his name so that his works would not be confused with publications of a similar vein written by his younger brother Séraphin Justin François Boex, or J.-H. Rosny jeune. J.-H. Rosny aîné is considered to be amongst the founders of modern science fiction.

8   Betz presumably refers to the alpine ranges above the valley of the Rhône and the region of the Valais where Rilke lived during the last years of his life at Muzot, and where, on 29 December 1926, Rilke died at the sanatorium of Val-Mont, perched above Montreux on Lake Geneva.

9   *Die Aufzeichnungen des Malte Laurids Brigge* or, as it was originally known, 'the journal of my other self', was Rilke's great prose work, published in 1910, translated by Betz as *Les Cahiers de Malte Laurids Brigge* and published in France in 1926, the year of Rilke's death. It is the book which Rilke and his French translator worked on together during the spring of 1925 in Betz's apartment near the Luxembourg in Paris, the memories of which are recounted in the pages of this book.

I. THE BOOK OF IMAGES, CIVILIZATION, 500,000 SHELLS

1   Rilke's *Das Buch der Bilder* was first published by Axel Juncker in 1902, the year Rilke moved to Paris to write a monograph on Rodin. It was extended and republished in 1906 to include work written between 1899 and 1905. Unlike the spiritual 'hymns' of *Das Stunden-Buch*, published in 1905, which caused Robert Musil to refer to Rilke as the most religious poet since Novalis, *The Book of Images* ushers in the new phase of Rilke's objectivity, the 'thingness' behind things, which was taken to its most developed phase in the *Neue Gedichte*, which followed in 1908.

2   *Le Canard enchaîné* (lit. 'The Chained Duck', or 'The Chained Newspaper') is a satirical weekly newspaper first published in Paris in 1915 during the First World War.

3   Maurice Barrès (1862–1923) was a French novelist, philosopher and politician. He is especially known for his trilogy of books titled *Le Culte du moi* influenced by Romanticism.

4 Maurice Barrès, *Chronique de la Grande Guerre*, 14 vols (Paris: Plon-Nourrit, 1920–24).
5 Georges Duhamel, *Vie et aventures de Salavin* (1920–32). Duhamel's five-volume novel revolves around the trials of a 'little man' in the twentieth century trying to come to terms with his salvation without the sustenance of religious faith.
6 Ernst von Wolzogen (1855–1934) was a cultural critic, novelist and founder of the German Cabaret.

II. DADA, MALRAUX, COCTEAU, HARDEN

1 Paul Claudel (1868–1955) was a French diplomat, poet, dramatist and younger brother of the sculptor Camille Claudel (1864–1943). Paul Claudel was best known for his verse plays, which treated deeply spiritual themes.
2 Betz's manuscript would be published as *Scaferlati pour troupes, poèmes suivis de La Malemort de Jean Lefranc* (Paris: A. Messein éditeur, 1921).
3 Ferdinand Florent Fels (1891–1977) was a prominent publisher and journalist who was particularly active in the art world and published books on painters, in the case of Van Gogh using *Les Contemporains*, the series so often quoted by Maurice Betz.
4 *Action* was a review of philosophy and art edited in Paris by Florence Fels and Marcel Sauvage, both writers and journalists. It was published in eleven issues from 1920 to 1922.
5 Henri Désiré Landru (1869–1922), nicknamed the Bluebeard of Gambais, was a French serial killer executed at the guillotine for his crimes.
6 Rainer Maria Rilke, *Duineser Elegien* (Leipzig: Insel, 1923). Rilke began writing the elegies in January 1912, after having been invited to Duino Castle near Trieste, Italy by his friend Princess Marie von Thurn und Taxis. Rilke would work on the elegies sporadically until the outbreak of the First World War, only completing them in February 1922 during his first autumn and winter at Muzot. The first English translation was published by the Hogarth Press, run by Virginia and Leonard Woolf, in 1931, translated by Vita and Edward Sackville-West.
7 Café de la Rotonde is an iconic café situated at 105, boulevard Montparnasse in Paris. Its inauguration in 1911 preceded that of its neighbours Le Select in 1925 and La Coupole in 1927. It was the café favoured by Picasso, being close to his studio on boulevard Raspail, and was particularly popular with painters thereafter.

8   André Malraux's novel *Les Conquérants* (1928) concerns the Guangzhou Uprising of 1927 in southern China.
9   Pierre Mac Orlan, *Malice* (Paris: Éditions Henri Jonquières, 1924).
10 At age nineteen the young writer and artist Maurice Eugène Clément 'Jean' Cocteau (1889–1963) lived at the Hôtel Biron, not only home to Rilke but also to Auguste Rodin, Henri Matisse, Isadora Duncan and Édouard de Max, amongst other artists and writers of the time.
11 Jean Cocteau, *Portraits-souvenir (1900–1914)* (Paris: Éditions Bernard Grasset, 1935).
12 Marcel Arland, *Terres étrangères* (Paris: NRF, 1923).
13 Maximilian Harden (1861–1927) was a journalist and spokesman for German nationalism before and during the First World War. He founded and edited the controversial weekly journal *Die Zukunft* (1892–1923).
14 Aline Mayrisch de Saint-Hubert (1874–1947) was a women's rights activist and philanthropist from Luxembourg.

III. FIRST LETTERS FROM MUZOT

1   During this period Rilke made two influential trips to Russia where he met Leo Tolstoy, L.O. Pasternak and Spiridon Drozhzhin.
2   Rilke was in Germany when war broke out in the late summer of 1914 and he was unable to return to Paris. His flat at 14, rue Campagne-Première was eventually emptied and many of his possessions were auctioned off or lost. But a small number were recovered by the tenacious efforts over the years of André Gide, and the box containing them was that which Rilke picked up from the then Gallimard offices at 3, rue de Grenelle on his first walk with Maurice Betz in February 1925.
3   Betz's first novel, *L'Incertain*, was published two years later by Émile-Paul Frères in 1925.
4   Betz is likely speaking of three of Rilke's poems that appeared in *Commerce* in the autumn of 1924: 'La Dormeuse', 'Eau qui se presse' and 'Salut! grain aile qui s'envole vers…'

IV. PARIS, THE FRENCH LANGUAGE, BERG AM IRCHEL

1   Auguste Rodin (1840–1917) was a monumental figure in Rilke's early years in Paris. The nature of the artist of genius and his lesson of unstinting work proved hugely influential, but their relationship was

corrupted when Rodin dismissed Rilke as his secretary over some petty error. They were reunited later, when Rodin gratefully moved into the Hôtel Biron where Rilke was already installed. But as Betz explains, this older Rilke had the measure of Rodin and the wreckage of his fraught human relations adjusted the former sense of devotion.

2 Baladine Klossowska (1886–1969) was a German painter and muse to Rilke, whom she met in Switzerland in 1919. Klossowska was with Rilke until his death in Muzot in 1926.

3 Lou Andreas-Salomé (1861–1937) was a Russian-born psychoanalyst who met Rilke in 1897 in Munich. Fourteen years his senior, Salomé was Rilke's advisor and confidante. She taught him Russian and changed his name from René to Rainer.

4 The Swedish artist and writer Ernst Norlind (1877–1952) met Rilke in Malmö in 1904.

5 The brothers Jérôme Tharaud (1874–1953) and Jean Tharaud (1877–1952) were French novelists and essayists who co-wrote under the name J.-J. Tharaud. Their writings focused on traditional Jewish life and Judaism and were often intended for a general French audience. The brothers would ultimately end up taking antisemitic views in their work.

6 This box, the vestiges of Rilke's possessions recovered from his apartment and saved from sale or dispersal by the tenacious efforts of André Gide, is that which Rilke finally collects from the then Gallimard office on rue de Grenelle during the first meeting and subsequent walk with Betz described later in Chapter VI.

7 At the end August 1902, at the age of twenty-seven, Rilke had gone to Paris to work on a monograph about Rodin. He stayed in a hotel on the rue Toullier just two blocks from the Jardin du Luxembourg.

8 Elisabeth von Schmidt-Pauli (1882–1956) was a German writer who wrote a number of biographies with religious themes. She also published a biography of Rilke in Basel in 1940. After her house was destroyed by bombing in the Second World War she retired to a monastery.

9 Elisabeth Maria Adelheid Dobržensky (1875–1951) was a Bohemian noblewoman who corresponded with a number of German-language writers including Robert Musil and Karl Kraus. She invited Rilke to come south from Berg am Irchel, Zurich in the summer of 1919 to stay in her chalet at Nyon on Lake Geneva.

V. ÉMILE-PAUL, JALOUX, BENVENISTE

1. Émile Paul was the founder of Émile-Paul publishing house, branded by his sons Albert and Robert Paul as Émile-Paul Frères.
2. *Les Nouvelles littéraires* was a journal of literature and art created in October 1922 and directed by Maurice Martin du Gard until 1936. In 1924 the journal also published a supplementary review, *L'Art vivant*. Though under another name the journal endured until 1985.
3. *La Petite Gironde* was a moderate republican daily newspaper in the south and south-west regions of France. It ran from 1872 to 1944.
4. The French poet and philosopher Pierre Morhange (1901–72) founded the journal *Philosophies* with Henri Lefebvre in 1932.
5. Pontigny is a commune in north-central France and the site of Pontigny Abbey. From 1910 to 1914 the philosopher Paul Desjardins held meetings at the abbey, known as 'Decades of Pontigny'. The meetings, or conferences, included such intellectuals and philosophers as Jean-Paul Sartre, Thomas Mann, Heinrich Mann, Nikolai Berdyaev and T.S. Eliot. After the end of the First World War, Desjardins again held meetings including such thinkers as Charles Du Bos, Roger Martin du Gard, André Gide and Paul Langevin, amongst others.
6. Countess Nora Purtscher Wydenbruck (1894–1959) was the niece of Rilke's close friend and patron Princess Marie von Thurn und Taxis, in whose castle at Duino on the Adriatic coast Rilke was staying over the winter of 1911–12 and where he was famously inspired to commence the *Elegies* which took its name.
7. Mme Gertrud Ouckama Knoop (1861–1931) was a German writer and chemist. Rilke dedicated his *Sonnets to Orpheus* to Knoop's daughter Wera, who died at age nineteen.
8. Fragments from the *Notebooks* were published in 1926 as 'Histoire de Nikolai Kousmitch (fragment inédit des *Cahiers de Malte Laurids Brigge*)', translated from the German by Maurice Betz, *La Revue européenne*, no. 38 (April 1926), pp. 13–18.
9. Founded in 1920, the *Revue de Genève*, after merging with *Bibliothèque universelle*, appeared until 1930. It was edited by Robert de Traz.
10. From mid-August to mid-September 1923 Rilke resided in Switzerland at the Sanatorium Schöneck bei Beckenried on Lake Lucerne, known in French as Lac des Quatre-Cantons (lit. four cantons), from the German Vierwaldstättersee (lit. lake of the four forested settlements).
11. Betz's autobiographical novel *Rouge et blanc* was published in 1923 by Albin Michel.

12 *Inouï* (unheard of/incredible/amazing); *unerhört* (incredible/tremendous/ outrageous); *ungehört* (unheard/on deaf ears).
13 *Cadenette* (long tress of hair); *fourragère* (military braid).
14 *Unbeirrbar* (unswerving/undeviating); *immuable* (immutable/unchanging); *imperturbable* (imperturbable/unshakeable).
15 *Muette* (speechless/silent).
16 '*Ils n'avaient de cesse que quand…*' (They only stopped when…).
17 Félix Arvers (1806–50) was a French poet and dramatist, known for his poem 'Un secret'.
18 Marthe Lucie Lahovary Bibesco, *Le Perroquet Vert par la Princesse Bibesco*, 1924.
19 Maurice Betz, 'Sur une crise de la conscience artistique', *Tendances—Les Cahiers du mois*, no. 1 (May 1924).

VI. LES CAHIERS DU MOIS, STERNHEIM, VALÉRY

1 The French periodical *Les Cahiers du mois* ran from 1924 to 1927 and was published by Émile-Paul Frères.
2 The phrase *la génération du mal du siècle* refers to the notion of a 'sickness' or world-weariness and malaise of mind experienced by the generation of youth living in early-nineteenth-century Europe. François-René de Chateaubriand would identify this malady, which was further described by Alfred de Musset in his *La Confession d'un enfant du siècle*. German Romantic author Jean Paul would use the term *Weltschmerz* (world-pain) for this sickness.
3 *Cahiers de la quinzaine* was founded by the French poet and philosopher Charles Péguy (1873–1914) in 1900. Amongst its contributors were Anatole France, Henri Bergson, Jean Jaurès and Romain Rolland.
4 Rainer Maria Rilke, *Reconnaissance à Rilke*, *Les Cahiers du mois*, no. 23/24 (1926).
5 Carl Sternheim, *Europa, Roman*, 2 vols (Munich: Musarion, 1919–20).
6 The German original of the French translation Betz refers to is *Busekow: Eine novelle von Carl Sternheim* (Leipzig: K. Wolff, 1914).
7 Robert de Traz, *Dépaysements* (Paris: B. Grasset, 1923). Robert de Traz (1884–1951) was a Swiss writer and part of the Neue Helvetische Gesellschaft (NHG)/New Helvetic Society movement which stemmed from the 1912 manifesto *Pro helvetica dignitate ac securitate* written by Traz, Alexis François and Gonzague de Reynold.
8 Rudolf Georg Binding (1867–1938) was a German writer and commander of dragoons in the First World War. His novel *Opfergang* was published in 1912.

9   The Hôtel Foyot was famous for its restaurant and accommodation on the rue de Tournon. In addition to Rilke, other writers such as H.D., T.S. Eliot, George Moore, Dorothy Parker and Raymond Radiguet were known to reside there. The hotel was demolished in 1937.
10 Balthus was modernist painter and Pierre a writer. Rilke helped Balthus publish a book of forty drawings titled *Mitsou*, which included a preface by Rilke.
11 Rilke had been living at 17, rue Campagne-Première in the Montparnasse area of Paris in 1914.
12 Eugène Carrière (1849–1906) was a French Symbolist artist of the *fin de siècle* known for his misty, monochromatic palette. Carrière was a close friend of Rodin.

VII. THE LUXEMBOURG, THE HÔTEL BIRON, MUZOT

1   The apartment of Maurice Betz was on the fifth floor at 1, rue Médicis facing the Luxembourg.
2   Rue Toullier was Rilke's first address in Paris, dating from 1902. It is from these cramped rooms that Malte, the narrator of the *Notebooks*, experiences in his first entry the overwhelming smells and sounds of the city.
3   From mid-May to July 1906 Rilke resided at 29, rue Cassette in Paris, and again from July to November 1907.
4   From mid-September to the end of October 1905 Rilke lived in Meudon with Rodin. He would live at Meudon again in early 1906.
5   In September 1908 Rilke resided at the Hôtel Biron on the rue de Varenne in Paris.
6   From the beginning of October 1902 through July 1903, Rilke resided at rue de l'Abbé de l'Épée whilst working on his book on Rodin. *Das tägliche Leben* and *Das Buch der Bilder* were published in 1902.
7   François Blondel (1705–74) was a French architectural engraver and designer. He taught and influenced prominent architects of his time and was the official architect for King Louis XV. His engravings were published in *De la distribution des maisons de plaisance et de la décoration des édifices en général* (1727–38).
8   The Duchesse du Maine, Anne Louise Bénédicte de Bourbon (1676–1753), lived at the mansion with its French-style garden which would later be known as the Hôtel Biron, located at 77, rue de Varenne.
9   *Paradou* is 'paradise' in the old *langue d'Oc* or language of Occitan, a region located in the Bouches-du-Rhône department in the south of France.

10 Aimée de Coigny was the subject and heroine of the famous eighteenth-century French poem 'La Jeune Captive' by André Chénier.
11 The poplar which Betz mentions was often cited by Rilke in spoken accounts and in correspondence to friends when he first moved into Muzot. Rilke saw it as a sort of symbol of anchorage, an announcement of his soon-to-be-rooted presence, an exclamation mark, a symbol of renewed application.
12 This reference to the Valaisan spring was another oft-repeated image dictated to correspondents, notably Antoinette de Bonstetten, Rilke's horticultural 'advisor' (see *Letters around a Garden*, Seagull Books, 2024). Rilke was fascinated by the suddenness of spring's arrival in the mountains and how it literally sucked or pulled the flowers out of the ground with an almost brutal disregard.
13 Emmanuel Bove (1898–1945) was a French writer (also under the pseudonyms Pierre Dugast and Jean Vallois). Colette helped him publish his first novel, *Mes amis*, in 1924 which received the Prix Figuière in 1928. Some twenty novels and collections of stories followed. Rilke rated him highly, as revealed in Betz's text.
14 *Valaisanne* is the name used to denote the Valais region. It can apply to the season, as here, or to an inhabitant of the Valais region; *une valaisanne* is a woman of the Valais.
15 From 1921 to 1926 Rilke lived in the thirteenth-century manor house Château de Muzot perched above the Rhône valley in the Valais. Here he found the long-sought-after refuge and fresh inspiration, enabling him to finally complete the *Duino Elegies*, abandoned since the war, as well as, in that highly productive year of 1922, receiving the unexpected gift of the *Sonnets to Orpheus*.

VIII. MORNINGS WORKING ON THE *NOTEBOOKS OF MALTE*

1 The Norwegian Symbolist poet Sigbjørn Obstfelder (1866–1900).
2 Rainer Maria Rilke, *Histoires du bon Dieu*, trans. Maurice Betz (Paris: Émile-Paul Frères, 1927). The first was published under the title *Vom lieben Gott und Anderes. An Große für Kinder erzählt* (Leipzig: Insel, 1900).
3 Rilke lived in his studio at Strohl-Fern Park in the winter of 1903–04.
4 Rilke's friend and supporter Ellen Key (1849–1926) was a Swedish feminist, psychologist and writer.
5 Rilke is referring to his prose poem *Die Weise von Liebe und Tod des Cornets Christoph Rilke*. The French edition, *Chant de l'amour et de la mort du Cornette*

Christophe Rilke, was translated by Maurice Betz and published by Émile-Paul Frères in 1940.

6   Rainer Maria Rilke, *Neue Gedichte* (Leipzig: Insel, 1908).
7   Rilke wrote *Das Stunden-Buch* in three parts between 1899 and 1903. It was published in 1905 by Insel Verlag.
8   In Les Baux-de-Provence during the Christmas vigil the master shepherd parades through village with his flock, culminating in an *aubade* (short concert) of tambourine players. The tradition dates back to the sixteenth century. The shepherds of Les Baux are mentioned in the chapter of *Malte* on the Prodigal Son, suggesting that he became one of their number.

IX. THE LOST PAGES OF *THE NOTEBOOKS OF MALTE*

1   Thebaid is a reference to the Theban desert entry in *The Notebooks of Malte Laurids Brigge* (*Die Aufzeichnungen des Malte Laurids Brigge*), trans. Stephen Mitchell (New York: Random House, 2011): 'A grand piano could have been built for you in the Theban desert… have streamed forth, unheard, giving back to the universe what only the universe can endure.'
2   The French term *Cour des miracles* (court of miracles) referred to slum districts of Paris where poor and homeless populations resided during the reign of Louis XIV (1643–1715).
3   The *Chroniques de Froissart* is a fourteenth-century prose history of the Hundred Years' War by Jean Froissart (1337–1405).
4   Lou Albert-Lasard (1885–1969) was a French Expressionist painter. She lived with Rilke in Vienna from 1914 to 1916.
5   *Les Annales—politiques et littéraires* was a popular cultural magazine in Paris in the early years of the twentieth century. It included writings on history, politics and literature but also carried articles on classical music and illustrated fairy tales.

X. IN THE ENVIRONS OF THE PRINCESS

1   Anna, Comtesse Mathieu de Noailles (1876–1933) was a French-Romanian writer whom Rilke read and admired. In 1921 she was honoured with the Grand Prix of the Académie française.
2   Clifford-Barney's *Aventures de l'esprit* was published by Émile-Paul Frères in 1929. Whenever she was in Paris, Natalie Clifford-Barney hosted a weekly international salon, receiving such figures as James Joyce, Ezra Pound, Isadora Duncan and Truman Capote. This collection of

reminiscences chronicles her friendships and associations and evokes the golden age of her salon.
3 Jacques Benoist-Méchin (1901–83) was a French journalist, historian and politician who served in the collaborationist Vichy government during the Second World War.
4 Raymond Schwab (1884–1956), French poet, editor and scholar.
5 The Théâtre des Petits Comédiens de Bois in Paris was one of a number of performances organized by Yulia (Julie) Sazonova featuring her wooden puppet troupes. This cultivated woman was also a writer, critic and historian of Russian theatre who had fled Russia after the Bolshevik Revolution in 1917, settling in Paris where she continued her métier and found a ready audience, Rilke amongst them. Puppets and dolls entranced him, for the reasons Betz cites here. Before the war in 1913 Rilke wrote a compelling essay after viewing the dolls of Lotte Pritzel at an exhibition in Munich.

XI. LOU ANDREAS-SALOMÉ, GORKI, TOLSTOY

1 Gricha Otrepjoff (False Dmitry, Grigory, Grishka, Dimitri, Pretender) was a runaway monk who in 1604 declared that he was Dmitry Ivanovich, the youngest son of Ivan the Terrible, and seized power in Moscow. In *The Notebooks of Malte Laurids Brigge* Rilke notes how the false Tsar was stabbed and thrown on a pile of corpses.
2 *Erlebnis* is the German philosophical term for experience, often translated as 'lived experience'.
3 Rilke met the Russian poet Spiridon Dmitryevich Drozhzhin (1848–1930) during the summer of 1900 whilst travelling with Lou Andreas-Salomé in Russia and was enthusiastic about his work.
4 Mikhail Yevgrafovich Saltykov-Shchedrin's (1826–89) novel *Les Messieurs Golovleff* was originally published in Russian in 1889 and concerns the Golovlyov family in Russia in the nineteenth century.
5 Ivan Bunin's works at that time would have included *The Village* (1910) and *Dry Valley* (1912), both short novels. His diary *Cursed Days* was published in 1926. Bunin was awarded the Nobel Prize in Literature in 1933.
6 The *kokoshnik* is a Russian headdress traditionally worn by married women. It was popular from the sixteenth to nineteenth centuries but dates back to the tenth century.
7 The term *moujik* is diminutive of the word *mouj*, or man, lit. manikin.
8 Yasnaïa Polyana is the former home of Leo Tolstoy, whom Rilke visited in 1900 on his second trip to Russia.

NOTES TO PAGES 105–10

9 Sofia Nikolaevna Schill was a Russian poet, journalist and translator. Rilke met her in Berlin through Lou Andreas-Salomé and she sent him a number of her books. Through Schill Rilke also obtained transcriptions of Chekhov's plays *The Seagull* (1896) and *Uncle Vanya* (1897).

XII. RODIN, DE MAX, ISADORA DUNCAN

1 Rilke met the young Countess Manon zu Solms-Laubach at the Villa Discopoli on the island of Capri, where he famously spent the winter and early spring of 1906–07. A correspondence ensued beyond their visit of some nineteen letters in Rilke's hand and he bestowed on her the gift of a calligraphic transcription of his famous poem 'The Panther'.
2 Judith Cladel (1873–1958) was a French playwright, novelist and biographer. She is the author of *Rodin, sa vie glorieuse, sa vie inconnue* (Paris: Bernard Grasset, 1936) and was instrumental in establishing the Musée Rodin in 1919.
3 Rose Beuret (1844–1917) was a French seamstress and laundress who was a long-time companion and muse of Auguste Rodin. She and Rodin married just weeks before her death in 1917.
4 La Beauce, the traditional bread basket of France, is a vast agricultural plain of arable crops which extends through the region of Loiret to the south-west of Paris.
5 The Duchesse de Choiseul (1864–1919) was Rodin's confidante and mistress, and for a time managed the sales and marketing of his work, especially in America.
6 Louise Charlin Perrin Labé (*c*.1524–66) was a French poet of the Renaissance.
7 Émile Verhaeren (1855–1916) was the most important Belgian poet between 1890 and 1914, as well as a prolific art critic and essayist. He was a force for European cultural integration and acted as a bridge in the arts between Paris and Brussels. Verhaeren's poetry spoke to Rilke at a profound level, and he read avidly the older poet's collections as they appeared during the period he lived in Paris up to 1914. Verhaeren, who also lived in Paris, met Rilke as early as 1905 through his position as Rodin's secretary. This led to a long correspondence and genuine devotion on Rilke's part. After the war and Verhaeren's death in an accident at Rouen station in 1916, Rilke made a special journey to see his widow Marthe in Paris.
8 Rilke, always prey to anxiety over his own poetry and its evolution, found in Verhaeren an anchorage, a stabilizing influence; alongside

the 'living' sculpture of Rodin, Verhaeren's vision offered a path to the modern.

9 *Les Villes tentaculaires* of 1895 dealt with the encroachment of industry on the rural Belgian landscape and the concurrent social concerns in a series of epic poems demonstrating the full scope of Verhaeren's wide-ranging poetic imagination, which tended to marry a febrile intensity with subtle perception; the whole underpinned by a sense of mourning for the vanishing past despite a faith in the creative energy aroused by technological invention. Rilke would have sensed elements sympathetic to his emerging *Notebooks of Malte*. Verhaeren's *Villes* established his reputation as a major European poet and a pioneer of modernism.

10 Maurice Maeterlinck (1862–1949) was a Flemish playwright and poet who wrote in French. In 1911 both he and Verhaeren were nominated for the Nobel Prize in Literature, which Maeterlinck duly won. He is best known in the English-speaking world for his popular play *The Bluebird* of 1908, which premiered at the Haymarket in London in 1910. But long before this, Maeterlinck's plays, prose and poetry had provided a conduit for the Symbolist epoch taking place on the continent. A biography by the English poet Edward Thomas was published by Chatto & Windus in 1912, and further collections of essays on the natural world and spiritual themes served to sustain Maeterlinck's reputation.

11 Eleonora Duse (1858–1924), also referred to as 'Duse', was a hugely influential and popular Italian stage actress and playwright. Rilke met with her frequently in Venice throughout 1912 (see Chapter XIV). Many writers adored her, wrote plays for her; in this cult of adoration Rilke was no different, but he, as no one else, saw the tragedy of her decline and its analogy of an old European/new American stand-off, which Betz delineates here with candour.

XIII. ROSES, CATS AND DOGS

1 Valery Larbaud (1881–1957) was a French writer, poet and prolific traveller, whose *brevet élémentaire de parisianité* tested the knowledge of those who thought they knew the French capital inside out. It is estimated that today only 0.1 per cent of Parisians would complete the test satisfactorily.

2 Balthus, *Mitsou. Quarante Images par Baltusz. Préface de Rainer Maria Rilke* (Leipzig: Rotapfel Verlag, 1921).

XIV. BETTINA VON ARNIM, LINA POLETTI AND ELEONORA DUSE

1. Bettina von Arnim, *Goethes Briefwechsel mit einem Kinde* (1835).
2. The antiquated German word *Backfisch* was common in the nineteenth century to describe adolescent girls.
3. The translation of the excerpt from the *Notebooks* is my own.
4. Lina Poletti (1885–1971) was an Italian poet, playwright and feminist. For a short time she was in a relationship with Eleonora Duse.
5. Gabriele D'Annunzio (1863–1938), Italian poet, novelist and playwright.
6. Eleonora Duse starred in Henrik Ibsen's play *A Doll's House* (1879), in which she played the role of Nora, as well as in *La Dame de la mer*, in Norwegian *Fruen fra havet*, which premiered in 1888.
7. Duse became ill whilst touring in the United States. She died in her hotel room in Pittsburgh, Pennsylvania, in April 1924.

XV. GIRAUDOUX, GIDE, MAX PICARD

1. Jean Giraudoux (1882–1944) was a major French playwright of the inter-war period who achieved international renown through his plays. He was also a novelist, essayist and diplomat. *L'École des indifférents*, one of some twenty collections of prose aside from the dramatic works, was published in 1911. Giraudoux was the first writer to be awarded the highest order of merit in France, the Légion d'honneur, in 1915.
2. In the nineteenth century asphodels carried the meaning 'remembered beyond the tomb', or 'my regrets follow you to the grave'. In Greek mythology they were associated with death and mourning.
3. Odilon-Jean Périer (1901–28) was a French-speaking poet and novelist from Brussels. He died of rheumatic pericarditis just short of his twenty-seventh birthday. In his short life he published several works including the poem 'Je vivais au milieu de choses mal unies', in which the quoted stanza appears.
4. Regina Ullmann (1884–1961) was a Swiss poet and writer. She corresponded with Rilke, who became a mentor to her. They first met in 1912. Ruth Schaumann (1899–1975) was a German poet, painter and sculptor.
5. Rilke greatly admired Paul Valéry and felt a spiritual bond with the French poet. Amongst the work he translated into the German are an impressive version of Valéry's famous poem 'Le Cimetière marin' (1921) and twenty-three poems from *Charmes* (between 1921 and 1923), which

were subsequently included in the collection *Paul Valéry, Gedichte* (Leipzig: Insel, 1925).
6 Max Picard was a Swiss writer and philosopher. His *Le Dernier Homme* appeared in 1923. Picard describes the modern individual fleeing from faith in a secularized and modern culture. Picard was one of the few writers at this time writing from a profoundly Platonic sensibility. One of his books, *Die Welt des Schweigens*, a moving rumination on the loss of silence in the modern age, has in recent English translation secured some attention in our present noisy world and kept Picard's name alive.
7 Friedrich Nietzsche's 'Last Man' in *Thus Spoke Zarathustra* is characterized by a life that lacks aspiration, avoids risk and seeks only security and comfort in material things, resulting in a culture of apathy and mediocrity. Nietzsche's foresight as to what would exist in the near future was thus uncannily accurate. The original *Also sprach Zarathustra: Ein Buch für Alle und Keinen* was originally published in four volumes between 1883 and 1885.

XVI. SPAIN, PROVENCE, VENICE

1 The annual Romani pilgrimage or *pèlerinage gitan* to the church of Saintes-Maries-de-la-Mer in the Camargue takes place over two days at the end of May. The festival to honour the black Madonna has been celebrated since medieval times and attracts thousands of Roma from across Europe.
2 Lucien Fabre, *Bassesse de Venise précédé de La Traversée de l'Europe en avion et du légat; avec un portrait de l'auteur par Man Ray gravé sur bois par G. Aubert* (Paris: Éditions de la Nouvelle Revue française, 1924).

XVII. 'FATE HAS THESE HOLES WHERE WE DISAPPEAR'

1 Rilke granted an interview to Lefèvre in the summer of 1925, published on 24 July 1926.
2 The Boeuf à la Mode was one of Paris's earliest restaurants, founded by the Méot brothers in 1792. It was the first dining establishment to offer an à la carte menu and offered *la bonne cuisine bourgeoise*, traditional home-style bourgeois cooking. It finally closed its doors in 1936.
3 Maurice Martin du Gard (1896–1970) was a French journalist, writer and editor of *Nouvelles littéraires*. Maurice Martin du Gard, 'Une heure avec Rainer Maria Rilke', *Nouvelles littéraires* (Paris, 1925).
4 *Der Türmer* was a monthly Protestant cultural journal on the right which first appeared in Stuttgart and then in Berlin from 1898 to 1943, which in

its heyday could shift 17,000 copies a month. It attacked democracy and the establishment, actively supporting the 'stab-in-the-back' conspiracy theory about the Jews having been responsible for the armistice with the Allied powers. Unsurprisingly, it was eventually taken over by National Socialists.
5   Maurice Betz, *L'Incertain*.
6   Emmanuel Bove, *Visite d'un soir* (Paris: Émile-Paul Frères, 1925).
7   Raoul Besançon, *Hélène aux remparts. Poèmes* (Paris: Picart, 1925).

XVIII. MALTE, VERGERS, RECONNAISSANCE À RILKE

1   The German translator, poet and publisher Witold Hulewicz (1895–1941) translated Rilke's work into Polish, in particular the *Duino Elegies*.
2   Rainer Maria Rilke's *Vergers: suivi des quatrains valaisans* was published in 1926 by *La Nouvelle Revue française*, which was part of the Gallimard house.
3   R.H. Heygrodt, *Rainer Maria Rilke: Die Lyrik* (Freiburg: Bielefeld, 1921).
4   'Aus dem Traum Buch' (1902 to 1907), in Rilke, *Prosa und Übertragungen* (Leipzig: Insel, 1942).
5   Rilke is likely speaking of Bove's 'Le Crime d'une nuit' published in *Les Œuvres libres*, no. 57 (1926).
6   The special issue of *Les Cahiers du mois* titled *Reconnaissance à Rilke* was published in the summer of 1926 and penned by Paul Valéry. See *Les Cahiers du mois*, no. 23/24, Paris.
7   Rilke translated twenty-three poems in *Charmes*, and translated the prose dialogue *Eupalinos ou l'Architecte* in *Eupalinos oder der Architekt Über die Architektur. Eingeleitet durch Die Seele und der Tanz* (Leipzig: Insel, 1927).

XIX. THE LAST SUMMER OF RAINER MARIA RILKE

1   This quote is from André Germain, *De Proust à dada* (Paris: Éditions du Sagittaire, 1924).
2   Amongst other works Rilke translated Valéry's *Fragments du Narcisse*.
3   Maurice Betz, *Le Démon impur* (Paris: Émile-Paul Frères, 1926). This was a departure from the earlier *L'Incertain*, a novel of manners in which Betz analyses the sensibilities and destinies of the young in his epoch. Rilke reacted positively to Betz in their correspondence concerning *L'Incertain*, but by its follow-up, *Le Démon impur*, which explored the incestuous love of a father, he was genuinely deeply impressed.

4 Nanny Wunderly-Volkart (1878–1962), whom Rilke fondly referred to in his letters as Niké, was a close friend and confidante of the poet during the final phase of his life in Switzerland.

RILKE ALIVE

1 *Letters to a Young Poet* is composed of ten letters Rilke wrote to a young cadet named Franz Xaver Kappus in 1903, when Kappus was nineteen. Kappus published the letters in 1929 following Rilke's death in 1926.
2 Inga Junghanns, whom Rilke met in Munich in 1915, was Rilke's Danish translator. She began working on the translation of *Malte Laurids Brigge* in 1917 and ten years later *Malte Laurids Brigges Optegnelser* was published by E. Jespersens Forlag in Copenhagen.

MORE RILKE FROM PUSHKIN PRESS

CHANGE YOUR LIFE: ESSENTIAL POEMS
*A selection of Rilke's most essential poems,
translated by acclaimed poet Martyn Crucefix*

DUINO ELEGIES
*The captivating original English translation of
Rilke's landmark poetry cycle, by Vita and Edward Sackville-West*

POEMS TO NIGHT
*A collection of Rilke's haunting, mystical poems of night
and darkness, appearing together for the first time in English
in a new translation by Will Stone*

RILKE IN PARIS
RAINER MARIA RILKE AND MAURICE BETZ
*A portrait of turn-of-the-century Parisian life,
art and culture by Rilke and his French translator*

CONVERSATIONS WITH RILKE
MAURICE BETZ
*Rilke's French translator offers readers a glimpse of the poet's
creative process, amidst the glittering cultural life of interwar Paris*

RILKE: THE LAST INWARD MAN
LESLEY CHAMBERLAIN
*An incisive, intimate account of the life and work of the
great poet, exploring his rich interior world*

AVAILABLE AND COMING SOON FROM PUSHKIN PRESS CLASSICS

The Pushkin Press Classics list brings you timeless storytelling by icons of literature. These titles represent the best of fiction and non-fiction, hand-picked from around the globe – from Russia to Japan, France to the Americas – boasting fresh selections, new translations and stylishly designed covers. Featuring some of the most widely acclaimed authors from across the ages, as well as compelling contemporary writers, these are the world's best stories – to be read and read again.

MURDER IN THE AGE OF ENLIGHTENMENT
RYŪNOSUKE AKUTAGAWA

THE BEAUTIES
ANTON CHEKHOV

LAND OF SMOKE
SARA GALLARDO

THE SPECTRE OF ALEXANDER WOLF
GAITO GAZDANOV

CLOUDS OVER PARIS
FELIX HARTLAUB

THE UNHAPPINESS OF BEING A SINGLE MAN
FRANZ KAFKA